A food revolution

OVER the past decade, Liverpool's food and drink scene has experienced a culinary renaissance with new restaurants emerging each week, putting Liverpool on the map as one of the premium places to eat out in the UK.

The region is bustling with cosmopolitan eateries offering exceptional cuisine and fine dining from the four corners of the gastronomic globe.

Whether you've got a craving for Afro-Carribean, a taste for Thai, or a penchant for Pan-Asian, you'll find it all here in the city which is home to Europe's oldest Chinese community.

At the helm of these restaurants are some of the most talented and passionate chefs in the country, putting their twist on classic and modern dishes with creative flair.

In creating our Liverpool Cookbook, we have tapped into their culinary talents, persuading them to share their favourite recipes with us, for you to try at home.

Taken from Michelin-starred chefs and chocolatiers to royal caterers, deli owners and ice-cream makers, there are dishes to suit every palate, spanning eateries from Church Street to the Lancashire and Cheshire borders.

And let's not forget to mention the food which made this city famous. We visit some of Liverpool's most treasured institutions, such as Maggie May's to find out how to make good old fashioned Scouse, as well as offering you a catch of the fruits of the Mersey with some sizzling seafood recipes.

Alongside mentioning the homegrown produce and sheep – from Formby asparagus, natural waters and Southport shrimps. There are also many food festivals showcasing the region's mouthwatering cuisine, including the hugely popular Liverpool Food and Drink Festival in Sefton Park, and Wirral Food and Drink Festival.

This book is a celebration of the finest fayre that Liverpool has to offer, with over 100 recipes from the city's top chefs, as well as lots of handy cooking tips and some fabulous photography. Enjoy!

Marco Pierre White

Swan

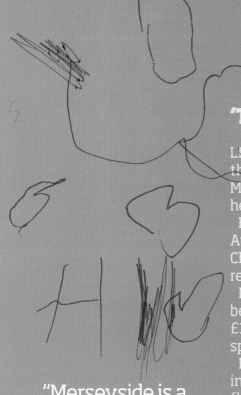

'The dining scene is thriving'

LIVERPOOL is now one of the most food savvy cities in the UK with celebrity chefs such as Jamie Oliver and Marco Pierre White, clamouring to set up restaurants here.

Having launched Marco Pierre White at the Swan Inn, Aughton, swiftly followed by Doubletree at Hilton Chester, the fiery Hell's Kitchen star is now opening a restaurant in Liverpool city centre.

Marco Pierre White Steakhouse Bar and Grill will become the focal point of Hotel Indigo, a brand new £15m boutique hotel in Chapel Street, due to open in spring 2011.

Marco says: "Merseyside is a fantastic place with an indelible link to international trade and an eclectic flavour of personalities to match.

"The dining scene here is thriving, with a handful of fine restaurants serving very good food, as well as a variety of top class producers.

Chapel Street stands testament to everything great about the city, from its glorious past to its bright future, and offers the ideal location for my latest venue."

At Jamie's Italian in Paradise Street, there is nearly as much Merseyside flavour as Mediterranean, with most of his 100 staff hailing from Liverpool, including head chef Paul Feery, formerly of Piccolino.

The crusading TV chef says he has always intended to come to the city but had been waiting for the right time before setting up shop on Paradise Place.

Jamie says: "Really Liverpool should have been our sixth Jamie's Italian but it ended up the eleventh because there was never the site that I wanted.

"To be honest the only debate was between Liverpool or Manchester so I asked my Scouse mates and I got a bit of an ear bashing.

"Now, with the buzz in the place, I know I made the right decision."

"Merseyside is a fantastic place with an indelible link to international trade and an eclectic flavour of personalities to match"

Heavenly delight

SHERRY TRIFLE WALLY LADD

Serves 6

18 discs of 5mm thick sponge
Chopped roasted almonds and pistachios
340g jar black cherry jam
150ml medium sherry
12 egg yolks
200g caster sugar
500ml whole milk
1 tbsp custard powder

For the crème Chantilly:
500ml double cream
100g caster sugar
3-4 drops vanilla essence

To whet your appetite, we bring you a classic dish from the Godfather of modern cooking. This take on a traditional dessert is one of Marco Pierre White's signature puddings. And it's a nod to Wally Ladd, a chef who worked at the Connaught in London some years ago.

Mix the jam and 100ml of the sherry in a pan and gently bring to the boil. Once the mixture has began to boil, allow to cool. Combine the egg yolks, sugar and custard powder in a bowl.

In a separate pan, bring the milk to the boil and pour over the egg mixture. Whisk together and return to the pan. Slowly cook the mixture over a low heat, stirring continuously until thick and allow to cool.

For the crème Chantilly, whisk the cream, sugar and vanilla essence in a bowl until it forms peaks.

To present the dessert, soak the sponges in the remaining sherry and spoon a little jam into six cocktail glasses. Place the sponge on the jam then layer the remaining sponges and jam until the glasses are filled up to 2.5cm from the top.

Spoon about 1cm of custard into each glass and add a layer of crème Chantilly on top and finish with a sprinkle of chopped almonds and pistachios.

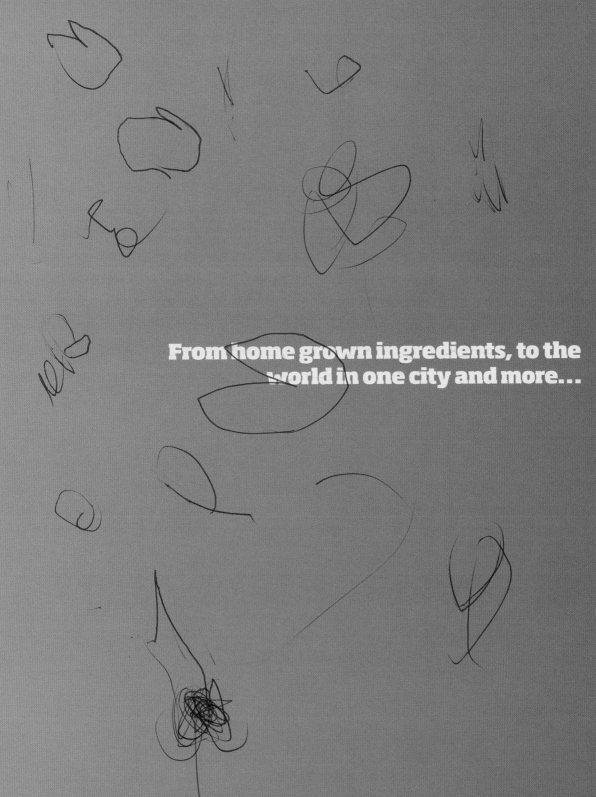

From home grown ingredients, to the world in one city and more…

TOP OF THE MENU

THE big city may not be synonymous with locally farmed food, but you may be surprised to find out that Merseyside's homegrown delicacies are making their way onto menus at many an eaterie . . .

Wirral Watercress

CHICKEN, MANGO & WATERCRESS SALAD

Wirral Watercress, based in Childer Thornton, has a reputation for producing high quality produce with a long shelf life. As the name suggests, the main product of the business is watercress, which is cut by hand on a daily basis and supplied to shops and restaurants across the region, from March until the end of December.

More recently, Wirral Watercress has been providing local chefs with microsalads as well as the watercress. Both the peashoots and the watercress were commended in the North West Fine Foods Awards 2008 and Wirral Watercress was awarded Merseyside Producer of the Year 2008.

Additional crops available according to their season include tomatoes, rocket, broad beans, runner beans, squash, courgettes and leeks.

Serves 4
50g asparagus tips
1 mango, peeled and stoned
100g red grapes
350g cooked chicken breast
1 bunch watercress
3 tbsp pumpkin seeds

For the dressing
1 orange, zest and juice
2 tsp dried chilli flakes
1 tsp honey
Salt and black pepper

Cook the asparagus tips in boiling water for 2 mins. Drain and refresh in cold water. Thinly slice the mango flesh and halve the grapes. Cut or tear the chicken into bite sized pieces. Place the asparagus, mango, grapes and chicken in a serving bowl. Add the watercress and pumpkin seeds.

Place all the dressing ingredients together in a bowl and whisk together with a fork. Drizzle over the salad and enjoy!

Leafy treat

This watercress dish is perfect for the summer and packed with nutrients. For the stock, a chicken stock cube is fine.

WIRRAL WATERCRESS SOUP

Serves 2

1 onion, finely chopped, 1 tbsp oil, 1 tbsp plain flour, 1 bunch of Wirral Watercress, 1 pint of stock

Fry the chopped onions in the oil till soft. Add the flour and mix well.

Add the stock slowly and leave to simmer for 3-5 minutes. Roughly chop the watercress and add to the stock. Simmer for a further 3-5 minutes.

Blend and serve immediately, topped with a spoon of crème fraîche.

WIRRAL, FORMBY AND CHESHIRE ARE BEST OF THE BUNCH

IF you're trying to keep your food miles down, then asparagus is the perfect summer vegetable for people living in the North West.

In Merseyside we're in prime position to get the very best of the British asparagus crop, with farms from Wirral, Formby and Cheshire offering excellent spears.

Producers of this local speciality have a high demand. In fact, when most of the peninsula was a royal forest, Henry VIII would come hunting his venison in the region and would indulge in the luxury of Wirral asparagus, as its sandy soil and sea air were perfect growing conditions.

Andrew Pimbley was much further afield when he became interested in growing asparagus at his family's farm in Spital. After a spell working in Australia, he returned to Wirral with the latest farming equipment and a passion for the unique vegetable.

"The climate here is perfect for growing asparagus, because of the sandy soil and the fact that we are on a peninsula, so it is cooler, allowing the asparagus to grow slower and thereby letting the flavour mature."

Andrew has 20 acres devoted to the crop at Claremont Farm and supplies many of Merseyside's top restaurants. At the launch of this year's asparagus season, Wirral's first tasty tips were rushed from farm to forks around the region, to Northcote in Blackburn, Fraîche in Oxton, and even to Pleasure Beach Resort, Blackpool, for the new Grill restaurant.

Michelin-starred chefs, Northcote's Nigel Haworth and Fraîche's Marc Wilkinson, pride themselves on sourcing fresh local produce, giving their diners the very best experience while also sustaining rural businesses in the community.

The season only lasts for a short time - from May to the middle of June - so enjoy local asparagus while you can!

Green spear hits home

ASPARAGUS HOLLANDAISE

Probably the best way to enjoy a plateful of fresh asparagus spears is to steam them and serve them with a pot of melted butter and a few grinds of fresh black pepper. But you can go further, providing you remember to keep the asparagus as one of the dominant flavours.

It loves dairy products, so soups and sauces work well. Perhaps one of the best friends to asparagus is the humble egg. Whether you simply rest a soft-poached hen's egg on top of some crunchy spears, or drizzle your plateful with a creamy hollandaise sauce, there is alchemy at work – the egg and the asparagus spear seem to be a match made in heaven.

To prepare, simply take a potato peeler and peel the bottom end of the stalk where the green starts to turn to grey, this is the tougher part. Plunge into some boiling salted water for a couple of minutes and serve with a vinaigrette or some wonderful olive oil and some parmesan shavings, or classically with hollandaise sauce, as here.

Serves 4
450g cooked asparagus
2 egg yolks
2 dessertspoons of warm water
250g melted unsalted butter
Juice of half a lemon
Salt and a pinch of cayenne pepper

To make the hollandaise sauce, place a bowl over a pan of hot water. Add the warm water and yolks and whisk until the colour lightens and the egg yolks have started to thicken. Slowly whisk in the butter little by little and, if necessary, remove the bowl occasionally from the pan of hot water. Add the lemon juice. And, lastly, season with salt and cayenne. Delicious served with lightly poached eggs.

Chef's tip
If the mix seems to be splitting, add a teaspoon of hot water to bring it back.

LIVERPOOL'S AWARD-WINNING FOOD CHAMPION

WITH a real desire to find the best produce, chef patron Paul Askew of The London Carriage Works has created a menu using locally sourced products wherever possible.

Liverpool's very own multi-award-winning food champion says: "I'm continually trying to find the best local produce and traceability is a big factor for us, we like to know where our food has come from.

"We can get vegetables picked at 6am, in the restaurant by 10am and serve them for lunch – our food is that fresh."

One of The London Carriage Works' main fruit and veg suppliers is Claremont Farm in Wirral.

Paul adds: "I regularly discuss suggestions with Andrew Pimbley at Claremont Farm, if I have new ideas I'll see if they're able to grow us certain vegetables for the following season, so each year we're getting better quality and traceability."

Other local suppliers include James Peet's Southport Potted Shrimps, sustainable fish from Liverpool and Birkenhead markets such as sea bass caught in Liverpool Bay, and a selection of top butchers.

Best of British

PAN-ROASTED WILD SCOTTISH HALIBUT WITH ENGLISH RISOTTO

Serves 2

2 x 200g steaks of wild halibut
200g blanched pearl barley
500ml fish stock
Half a glass of dry white wine
1 leek
1 clove of garlic
1 large shallot
50g mature Kirkham's Lancashire cheese
Flat leaf parsley
2 spring onions
50ml double cream
Maldon or Kosher salt
Freshly cracked black pepper
Fresh green salad
Cherry tomatoes
Thyme
Olive oil
Unsalted butter and vegetable oil

Paul Askew suggests serving this dish with a Menetou Salon 'Clos des Blanchais' Henry Pelle 2007 – enjoy!

To prepare, blanch the pearl barley in salted water for 10 minutes, until almost done. Wash and dice the leek, peel and chop the shallot and peel and dice the garlic. Chop the spring onions and parsley and grate your cheese.

Put a non-stick thick bottom frying pan on the stove to heat up. In another saucepan, start the risotto, put in a little butter and oil and sauté the leeks, shallot and garlic for 2 minutes then add the cooked pearl barley and 4 tbsp of stock and half of the wine. For the risotto, fresh fish stock is best but a stock cube will do!

While this is cooking, season the fish on both sides with Maldon or Kosher salt and put a splash of oil in the hot pan, place the fish immediately into the hot pan.

Caramelise the fish on one side then turn it over allowing it to brown on the other side, then add a little butter to finish. Allow the fish to rest for a further two minutes. Don't be tempted to overcook the fish.

To finish the risotto, add the double cream, seasoning, parsley, spring onions, stirring all the time, then finally the cheese.
If a little more stock or wine is needed for consistency and balance, do so and check seasoning before serving.

Serve in a pasta bowl, risotto at the bottom, fish on top, garnish with some nice green salad and some cherry tomatoes roasted in thyme and olive oil.

Traditional and tasty

LANCASHIRE HOTPOT

Nigel Paul Smith has always been a fan of celebrating local produce and traditional cooking techniques.

The executive chef at Liverpool's Maritime Dining Rooms, located on the fourth floor of the Merseyside Maritime Museum, ensures every dish on its new menu carries his passion for all things British, especially in his meat main courses. Through the restaurant's butchers, Althams of Morecambe, Derbyshire-born Nigel and his team are able to source the finest local pieces of meat keeping the carbon footprint down and supporting local producers.

Here he offers up a very local treat. Says Nigel: "Lancashire hotpot is one of my all-time favourites and probably one of the best known dishes from the area. It's also one of the hardest to master because everyone has their own little tweak in what they do to the original recipe to make it their own."

Serves 4
900g lamb neck chops or fillet
A few sprigs of thyme
40g diced turnip
40g diced celeriac
60g diced carrot
500ml chicken stock
2 large onions, sliced
1 star anise
50g butter
500g potatoes

For the red cabbage
1 head of red cabbage (400-450g)
2 star anise
400ml red wine
275 ml malt vinegar
140 ml white wine vinegar
140 ml balsamic vinegar
5 bay leaves
10 whole cloves
1 tsp whole black peppercorns
1 tsp whole pink peppercorns
1 stick cinnamon - snapped in half
5 whole dried red chillies
300g caster sugar
55g coarse sea salt - for salting the cabbage

Trim excess fat from the lamb and sauté to get a rich colour, seasoning well. Set aside.

Sauté the onions in butter with the star anise and cook until without colour, when very soft remove from the heat. Sauté the turnip, celeriac, carrot and thyme to get a nice colour then deglaze with chicken stock to cook them through. Slice your potatoes into discs and line them in a ceramic or cast iron pot.

Place one quarter of the diced vegetables in the bottom, then one eighth of the onion, then the sliced lamb. The next layer is onion, potato, lamb and the final layer is potato. This needs to be arranged more tidily as this is the presentation layer. As you go through building the layers, season and top up with stock as neccessary, adding a few flecks of butter here and there to the potatoes.

Cook in an oven at 180°C for about 90 minutes or until the potato is golden brown.

For the red cabbage

This should be made at least a day in advance. Halve and quarter the red cabbage. De-vein away the large stem and finely slice the red cabbage leaves (alternatively put through a food processor). Salt the cabbage well in a colander for two hours until a deep rich colour is achieved. Rinse and wash all the salt away thoroughly, then pat dry. Place all the vinegars, wine and sugar in a suitable pan and reduce by half. Place all the dry ingredients in a pestle and mortar and coarsely pound. When the reduction is near completion place all the dry spices into the reduction and allow to infuse for five minutes. Pass the reduction through a fine sieve and while hot pour onto the red cabbage in a suitable jar. Allow cooling, leaving the red cabbage out overnight. Refrigerate. Serve up with the hotpot as the perfect accompaniment.

A MAN FOR ALL SEASONS

DELIA SMITH is the oracle of the British kitchen.

When she speaks the nation listens – and one beneficiary is a Merseyside spice emporium.

Wirral-based Seasoned Pioneers have been bringing a taste of the exotic to our kitchens for nearly eight years. The company has a legion of celebrity fans – including Nigella Lawson, Antony Worrall Thompson and Rick Stein.

But when Delia Smith followed suit and promoted 10 of the firm's products in her book and TV series, How To Cheat At Cooking, sales went through the roof.

"Delia came to film with us and was lovely," says founder Mark Steene, from Toxteth. "She's not starry at all. She's really passionate about food, and loved what we do. She featured 10 different products, more than any other producer in the series, and we're really grateful to her."

Mark started the company after he got a taste for authentic spices while back-packing around Asia.

Unable to buy the same ingredients at home, he began to import spices and mix them in his city flat. Before long he was selling his blends to friends,

and then local delicatessens. Now the company has premises in Bromborough but still uses only traditional production methods – dry roasting and hand blending.

"All our products are made from authentic spices," he explains. "Customers can either choose to do everything themselves, roasting, grinding and choosing their own mixtures, or they can buy a blend. I don't see that as cheating. It's just about making the choice available.

"Even the most dedicated foodie and culinary enthusiast wants – or needs – a night off from the kitchen, especially after a busy day.

"We also do gourmet cooking sauces, so it's simple to recreate authentic international dishes at home, and your meal is ready in less time than it would take to find the take away menu."

The Seasoned Pioneer range includes Shrimp Paste (Thai Kapee), Tandoori Masala, Cardamom Masala, Tamarind Paste, Tsire Powder, Indonesian 'Seven Seas' Spice, Poudre De Colombo Spice Blend, Ras-el-Hanout Spice Blend, Sambhar Powder, Goan Xacuti Curry Powder.

Spicy and sweet
COLOMBO CURRY

This Caribbean-style Colombo curry uses Seasoned Pioneers' Poudre de Colombo spice blend and has a spicy flavour with sweet lemon notes.

Serves 4

3-4 tsp Seasoned Pioneers' Poudre de Colombo Spice Blend
4 white fish fillets, 3 tomatoes, 1 onion, 1 green pepper
2 tsp fresh basil leaves, ½ tsp crushed black peppercorns
2 tsp thyme, 2 finely chopped garlic cloves, 5cm piece ginger root
125ml lemon juice, ½ tsp sea salt, 3 tsp sugar to taste, 3 tbsp peanut oil

Rinse and dry the fish thoroughly then sprinkle with salt, pepper and lemon juice. Set aside. Finely slice the tomatoes, chop the onion and green pepper, and finely slice the ginger root.

In a frying pan, heat oil until hot. Add the garlic and sauté.
When soft, add the green pepper and onion and sauté until soft. Mix in the Poudre de Colombo, tomato and basil. Cook for 10 minutes, uncovered. Add the ginger, sugar and thyme and cook for a further 10 minutes. Add the fish fillets, cover and cook on a low heat for 10 minutes. Serve hot.

PICKLED WALNUT

BESPOKE catering company Pickled Walnut likes to serve its food with fun and flourish!

Launched in 2005 by Liverpool chefs Jamie Anderson and Mark Kershaw, the company has really made its mark on the catering scene in the North West.

Dedicated to using locally sourced ingredients, Jamie says: "We should always look to use local produce and embrace the region's food heritage. Let's all do our part in putting British food back on the dinner table."

Nuts for originality

ORANGE INFUSED BALLOTINE OF SALMON

Pickled Walnut's signature dishes are centred around British classics with a twist. Their customised recipes, combined with a touch of theatrical presentation, have ensured they are the caterer of choice for a whole variety of high profile receptions throughout the region.

Jamie Anderson says: "For the ideal way to start off our meal we have chosen one of our signature dishes - orange infused ballotine of Fleetwood Salmon, served with salmon roe and coriander crème fraiche. It has been with us since we started five years ago and although it has evolved over time, with the additions of modern trends, the core of the dish remains a well cooked moist salmon served with a flavoured crème fraiche and acidic syrup."

Makes 10-12 pieces

Ballotine
2 x 600g filleted and trimmed sides of salmon
4 oranges (zested and juiced)
30g sugar
Cayenne pepper
Salt
1 gelatine leaf
Chopped dill, parsley and tarragon
1.5 litres of milk and water for poaching

Coriander crème fraiche
300g crème fraiche
Chopped coriander

To garnish:
2 oranges, segmented
4 radishes cut up into matchsticks
1 jar of salmon roe (also known as caspian pearls)
Microleaves (1 punnet)

Soak the salmon with the cayenne pepper, salt, orange zest and juice for 24 hours. Remove the salmon from the marinade and pat dry. Put one side of salmon, skin side down, on a piece of cling film. Cut the gelatine into equal strips and place along the salmon, then top with the second side of salmon, skin side up. Roll the salmon in clingfilm to make a perfectly even sausage and tie tightly at both ends.

Poach, just covered in hot salted water, for five minutes per kg, turning a half turn at the midway point. Remove from the heat and allow to rest in the liquid for a period equal to the cooking time. Add enough ice to cool rapidly, then remove from the liquid and refrigerate overnight. Carefully remove the clingfilm and roll the ballontine in the chopped herbs. Wrap again tightly in clingfilm and reserve to slice until ready.

To make the orange syrup, take the orange juice from the marinade, add 30g of sugar and reduce to a syrup. For the coriander crème fraiche, add the chopped coriander to the crème fraiche. To assemble the dish, carve the salmon and garnish as your mood takes you.

The wow factor

WELSH LAMB DUO

Jamie Anderson of Pickled Walnut shares his recipe for a duo of Welsh lamb – confit shoulder, roast chump, shallot purée, fondant potatoes, and a red wine jus.

Jamie says: "This dish is the perfect addition to a night in, whether you're entertaining 2 or 200, it can be replicated by any home cook and provides a rich and flavoursome dish which will wow your guests. The dish is labour intensive but can be prepared in advance and is definitely worth the extra care it takes to prepare. Serve with some best fine beans and a nice new world pinot noir."

Serves 4

Confit Shoulder
1kg shoulder of Welsh lamb (boned and laid out)
2 sprigs of rosemary and thyme
Sea salt (for the rub)
Black pepper for seasoning
2 cloves of garlic
Zest of 1 lemon
1 litre duck fat

Puree
10 banana shallots
100ml cream
50g butter

Fondant Potatoes
4 Maris Piper potatoes
200g butter
Salt and pepper
600ml chicken stock
Thyme

Red Wine Jus
250 ml dry red wine
125ml beef stock
125ml lamb stock
2 cloves of garlic
1 sprig of fresh rosemary

Confit Shoulder

The important thing is to start this the day before by pricking holes in the lamb with a small paring knife and pushing chopped up garlic and sprigs of thyme inside. Once that's done it is time to rub the rock salt into the meat – distribute evenly throughout (this will draw out some moisture from the meat). Place in a casserole dish big enough to lay the meat out flat and add the lemon zest and the remaining rosemary and thyme. Season with black pepper and cover with the duck fat.

Put the dish on a flame on top of the stove until it comes to a tepid boil and place a lid on top. Put in the oven on around 120°C (this will take approximately 3 and a half hours, but ovens vary so check it every hour by taking it out and piercing the meat with a small knife) Once cooked, remove the meat from the fat and press it between 2 loaf tins and leave to set overnight in the fridge, once it is cool enough to do so.

Chump of Lamb

2 good sized chumps should do this recipe. Simply pan fry the meat fat side down with olive oil and season with salt and pepper. Cook for around 7 minutes (depending on the size of the lamb) and rest for 4 minutes. Put back in the pan for 2 minutes or until the lamb is cooked pink/medium rare. Carve length-ways to get lovely long slices of succulent meat (important to do this just before serving to avoid dry, grey meat).

Shallot Puree

Roast the shallots in an oven inside the skins for approximately 25 mins at 230°C (or until they are lovely and soft). Once cooked, squeeze the onion flesh out of the skins into a food processor and blitz until velvet smooth. Season with salt and white pepper. Transfer to a pan, add the cream and stir until you have the right consistency. Add the butter at the end and check the seasoning.

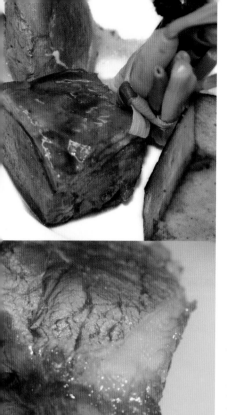

Fondant Potatoes

Cut the butter into thin slices on the bottom of an oven proof tray. Peel and cut the potatoes into rustic ovals and place on the butter (it is important they are all the same size). Place on top of the stove and wait for the butter to sizzle (this will seal the potatoes). When the butter is about to brown, add the seasoning, thyme and stock and place in the oven for 20 minutes on 180°C. The stock should reduce down and absorb into the potatoes. Serve the side that has been face down in the butter as it will be a lovely golden brown.

Red Wine Jus

Grab a small saucepan and put it over a low heat. Break 2 garlic cloves with the flat side of your knife and drop them into the saucepan. Pour in the wine and submerge the rosemary sprig. Let the red wine simmer with the herbs over a medium heat until the volume has reduced by half. This should take about 20 minutes. Give it a swirl around the pan every 10 minutes to combine. Once reduced, pour in the beef and lamb stock along with a couple of turns from your pepper grinder. Again, let the sauce reduce by half over a medium heat for about another 20 mins, let it simmer, but not boil. Leaving it on a lower heat for longer will give you a much more concentrated sauce. Strain through a fine sieve or just spoon out over the confit lamb as the dish is finished.

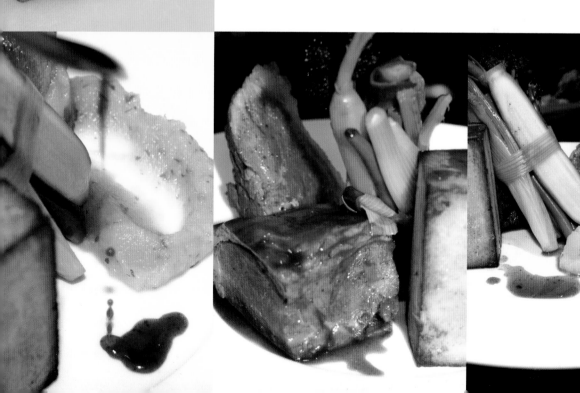

A real Liverpool trailblazer

BRAISED BEEF IN CAINS BEER PIE

Paul Heathcote was the first celebrity chef to blaze a trail improving the culinary offerings of Liverpool.
Already an established name with his then Michelin-starred Heathcote's at Longridge near Preston, he opened Simply Heathcotes in Beetham Plaza in 2001. Paul now has an extensive restaurant portfolio around the country, including the modern Italian eaterie the Olive Press in Castle Street, Liverpool.

He is also the culinary force behind ACC Liverpool. The award-winning Heathcotes Outside team has catered at the ECHO Arena and BT Convention Centre for events like BBC Sports Personality of the Year and the MTV Europe awards. In 2009, Paul was recognised for his services to the hospitality industry with an MBE.

Makes 12
1.2 kilo of braising steak
Sea salt
Vegetable oil
6 carrots
3 small onions
1 clove garlic
1 bay leaf
Sprig of thyme
10g sugar
75ml red wine vinegar
125ml red wine
200ml Cains beer
36 soft green peppercorns
2 pints beef stock
A little corn flour dissolved
A few drops of gravy browning if necessary

Shortcrust Pastry (8 portions)
300g soft baking flour
A good pinch of salt
75g butter
75g lard or vegetable fat
4-6 tbsp water

Dumplings
Half a medium onion
120g self raising flour
60g beef or vegetable suet
Small bunch of parsley, roughly chopped
Half a teaspoon English mustard
80ml water
Sea salt and pepper

Cut the braising steak into chunks. Season the meat with salt and brown in oil until golden brown all over. Peel the carrots and cut into big chunks. Add to the pan with half of the onions, quartered, followed by the sugar and caramelise. Deglaze with vinegar followed by red wine.

Add the beer, bring to the boil and add the stock. Cook for about 1 hour 45 minutes, at about 160°C, until very tender.

Remove the beef, lift out the carrots and onions carefully and reserve to one side, pass the remaining liquor through a sieve and bring to the boil, add the peppercorns and a few drops of corn flour if necessary and gravy browning possibly for colour.

Place the beef and vegetables into a pie dish with a couple of dumplings, fill with the gravy and cover with pastry. Brush with milk and bake at 170°C until brown for about 20 minutes.

Shortcrust Pastry
In a bowl mix the flour and salt together, add both the butter and fat with the palm of your hands and rub into a fine crumb. Add sufficient water to make a firm paste but it is important to do this gently. Rest for half an hour before rolling out and use for covering the pies.

Dumplings
Finely chop the onion and boil in just enough water to cover for about one 1 minute, drain well. Mix the flour and suet together, add the parsley, roughly chopped, and mustard and bind together with the water. Season with sea salt and freshly milled pepper and roll about 3-4cm long.

Cut into 2cm thick rounds, they are ready to bake.

Local starters ordered at Aintree

CREAM OF ORMSKIRK SOUP

For thousands of race-goers, the Grand National is a time to pull on their glad rags and spend some hard earned cash having a flutter on the horses.

And with a grand day out comes some grand eating and drinking. The chefs at Aintree have to cater for all when preparing the menu for the three-day event, and the man given the task of ensuring that is Richard Busfield, Aintree Racecourse's regional executive chef. Richard, who has been involved with food production and menu development for the Grand National at Aintree for 12 years says he has devised each menu with the focus on fresh produce.

"One of the starters is cream of mushroom soup and it was only when we were looking to source the mushrooms that we discovered the farm was just down the road in Ormskirk, hence the name cream of Ormskirk soup. This is a creamy, hearty soup full of fresh ingredients," says Richard.

Serves 4
50g butter
100g mushrooms, sliced
1 onion - half chopped finely and the other half sliced
1 clove garlic, chopped finely
2 sticks of celery
Half a leek
1 vegetable stock cube
50g flour
140ml of double cream

Gently cook the chopped onions, garlic, celery and leeks until soft. Add half of the sliced mushrooms and cook a little longer. Add the flour then the vegetable stock, bring to the boil and cook for about 20 minutes until smooth. Add double cream and season to taste.

In a separate pan, sauté the sliced onions and the rest of the mushrooms until cooked, add this mix to the soup just before serving.

Serve with a warm bread roll.

A fab final hurdle

CHOCOLATE MUFFIN WITH BAKED PEAR

Makes 12

150g dark chocolate, chopped
110g butter
450g all purpose flour
110g brown sugar
2 tsp baking powder
Half tsp salt
2 large eggs
Two thirds of a cup of buttermilk (about 160ml)
1 tsp vanilla extract
1 cup chocolate chunks - dark or semisweet
1 baby pear per person
1 tin of pears
Icing sugar

The desserts at Aintree have people licking their lips and leave them full to bursting – here we have a traditional dark chocolate muffin, served with a baby baked pear and mint choc chip ice cream.

Heat the oven to 180°C. Line a 12 hole muffin tin with paper muffin cases. Put the chocolate and butter in a heatproof bowl. Microwave on medium (500W) for 2 minutes, stir and microwave for two more minutes until smooth (alternatively, rest the bowl over a pan of gently simmering water). Stir together the flour, baking powder, bicarbonate of soda, cocoa powder and golden caster sugar in a large bowl.

In a jug, lightly mix together the buttermilk and eggs. Pour into the dry ingredients with the melted chocolate mixture. Mix together until just combined. Divide the mixture between the prepared paper cases and bake the muffins for 18 minutes until risen and firm.

Cut a heart shape out of a piece of paper, rest paper over a muffin and dust with sieved icing sugar. Serve with one scoop of mint choc ice cream and a baked baby pear on a bed of puree, made by putting the tinned pears through a blender.

29

MAGGIE MAY'S

SCOUSE is as synonymous with Liverpool as Jersey Royal potatoes and Cornish clotted cream are with their regions.

Liverpool's favourite dish has been on the menu at Maggie May's ever since John Lea started the business with his wife, Sue, 16 years ago.

Maggie May's was featured on the BBC programme Michael Portillo's Great British Railway Journeys. Mr Portillo ate every spoonful and said it tasted "like ghoulash." He loved it and said next time he was in the city he would come back for another bowl. The meal has proved so popular that it's even available in tins to take away.

John, who started out as a caterer on cruises and ferries, before setting up a home from home in Bold Street, says: "Everyone makes Scouse differently - this is just my recipe, which is based on the way my mum made it."

Our dish
SCOUSE

Scouse was first brought to Liverpool by Norwegian sailors and called labskause. During the 19th century, its name became Anglicised and evolved to lobscouse and then finally Scouse. The original recipe was much simpler than some of its modern variants, but was predominantly the same staple ingredients - meat, vegetables and potatoes. After a day stewing in the kitchen, an authentic portion of Scouse should allow the spoon to stand straight up in the bowl.

Serves 6
900g of Welsh Black Beef
2kg of potatoes (preferably King Edward) peeled and cubed
2 pints of beef stock
2 large white onions
4 large carrots, peeled and diced
Tomato puree
Salt and pepper

Seal the beef in a large pan adding onions and carrots. Add 1 pint of beef stock, bring to the boil.

Add the potatoes, peeled and cubed, then cover with the other pint of beef stock.

Add about half a tube of quality tomato puree. Add salt and pepper to taste. Leave to simmer for 4 hours until the Scouse is completely cooked and blended together.

Timeless scran

PEA WACK SOUP
WET NELLY

Liverpudlians are famous for being creative – especially when it comes to food or 'scran', as we affectionately call it. Scouse goes without saying – but there's also Pea Wack soup which has given us another nickname in 'Wackers'. This heart-warming meal is one of the top-sellers at Maggie May's eaterie, as is the pudding Wet Nelly.

John Lea, manager of Maggie May's says: "I have friends called Pea Wack – just as soldiers and sailors were called Scousers. Liverpool people were always inventive when it came to using war time rations.

"As for Wet Nellies I just love the name – it conjures up something mysterious and yet typically Liverpool – a bit surreal. What other city could have a musical written by Brian Jacques at The Everyman Theatre called 'Brown Bitter, Wet Nellies and Scouse'? "What a pity they couldn't get Pea Wack in the title, but then it would sound like a menu on the posters.

"Wet Nellies were big in Great Homer Street and generations still talk about them, and happily still eat them. Just like Scouse, they are timeless, belly-filling dishes."

Serves 4-6
For the Pea Wack
3 rashers of smoked, rindless, streaky bacon, diced
1 large onion, chopped
Small knob of butter
450g of ready soaked peas
225g cubed York Ham
4 pints of chicken stock
5 floz double cream
Chopped parsley
Salt and freshly milled black pepper

Pea Wack

Put the bacon and onion into a large saucepan with a little butter and cook over a gentle heat for 4-6 minutes.
Add the peas, ham and the stock to the pan, bring to the boil, season lightly with salt and pepper.
Cover and simmer for 2 hours.
Add the cream and blend thoroughly, sprinkle with parsley.

Serves 6-8
For the Wet Nelly
450g of shortcrust pastry
225g trifle sponges
100g raisins
Grated rind and juice of one lemon
4tbsp of milk
100g of golden syrup
Milk and caster sugar to glaze

Wet Nelly

Set the oven at Gas Mark 5/190°C.
Line an 18cm/7in sandwich tin with the pastry.
Break up the trifle sponges into breadcrumbs. Mix together the sponge crumbs, raisins, lemon rind, lemon juice, milk and syrup.
Place the mixture in the pastry case. Roll out the remaining pastry and cover the filling.
Seal and trim the edges. Brush with a little milk and sprinkle with caster sugar.
Bake in the pre-heated oven for 30 to 40 minutes.

CRAIC OPEN REAL IRISH SPIRIT

MILLIONS of people around the world – some Irish, some of Irish descent, some who feel Irish and some who just like Guinness – unite in celebrating St Patrick's Day.

And there are always plenty of pints raised and then downed in Liverpool, which has such close links with Ireland.

More than 1.3m Irish people passed through the gates of Clarence Dock in Liverpool as they fled the Irish famine during the mid-19th century. Today, a plaque at the dock commemorates those who entered the country through Liverpool between 1845 and 1852.

It has been estimated that up to 50% of Liverpool people have an Irish background, and, in the eyes of many, Liverpool is the spiritual capital of Ireland – not Dublin; although Dublin shouldn't take offence – it is, after all, one of our twin cities. In fact, as the crow flies, Dublin is closer to Liverpool than Cork – Ireland's second biggest city.

Wherever you go in Liverpool, the influence of the Irish community can be felt, affecting everything from the Scouse accent to politics, literature, music, food and drink. If you're looking for some tasty Irish stew or a good pint of Guinness, you are spoilt for choice in Liverpool.

We make other cities green with envy.

Delivered fresh from Ireland

SALMON & COLCANNON FISHCAKES

"In the last few years people have become more and more interested in traditional Irish food," says Eamonn Lavin, manager of O'Neill's in Liverpool.

Eamonn, originally from Dublin, adds: "They want authentic recipes and high-quality ingredients. We're really proud of the provenance of the food served at O'Neill's, as many of our key ingredients are sourced from Ireland.

"O'Neill's Irish steaks are high quality and full of flavour; they come from grass-fed Irish cows and are matured for at least 21 days. We also serve prime Irish pork and herb sausages, Irish Cheddar, Cashel Blue cheese from Tipperary and soda bread from Irwin's bakery in Northern Ireland. The dessert menu features Irish Bramley Apple tart and Silver Pail Irish ice cream. Even the tea and coffee are Irish, as we source them from Bewley's, Ireland's leading tea and coffee company."

Serves 4-6

500g raw salmon
(boneless and skinless)
500g potatoes
125g Savoy cabbage
Half tsp salt
Quarter tsp pepper
15g white wine
1 egg (beaten) for coating
Dried white bread for crumbing

Peel and chop the potatoes into even-sized chunks and bring them to the boil – cook until tender. Thinly shred the Savoy cabbage and boil for 4-5 minutes. For best results, chill the cabbage after boiling. Lay the salmon in a frying pan and pour in 1 pint of water to cover. Bring the fish to the boil and cook for about 8-10 minutes. Take off the heat and let it stand for another 5 minutes and then drain.

Place the boiled potatoes into a bowl and mash with a fork.
Add seasoning and white wine to the mashed potatoes.
Next fold in the salmon and shredded Savoy cabbage to the seasoned mashed potato and mix well.
Divide and shape the fish cake mix into 8-10 portions.

Dip the fishcake mix in egg and coat in the breadcrumbs.
Chill for 30 minutes before frying.

Fry the fishcakes in hot oil for 3-5 minutes until golden brown and thoroughly heated.

Take it slow at The James Monro

IRISH STEW

Everyone has their own way of making Irish stew – and your mum's is usually the best – but The James Monro on Tithebarn Street gave us a recipe with a twist which includes the famous black stuff.

Named after the first scheduled passenger service to New York in 1817 direct from Liverpool, The James Monro, specialises in both contemporary and heritage dishes from both sides of the ocean.

Chef Leigh Harvey says: "This is a slow cooking dish which would have been cooked on the embers of a peat fire over night and eaten the next day. In this fast world though it's easy to forget how flavoursome slow cooking can be, so give this Irish stew a try over the weekend."

Serves 4
1 can Guinness - half for the pot, half for the cook!
2 large onions
1.5lbs neck of lamb (best end), cut into cutlets and trimmed - get your butcher to advise/do this
1lb potatoes
2 tbsp fresh parsley, chopped
1 tsp thyme
Salt and pepper
300-400ml vegetable stock (Swiss Bouillon is best)

Preheat oven to 170°C/gas mark 3.

Peel and dice the onions. Peel and slice the potatoes.

In a casserole dish, layer the lamb, onions and potatoes. Between each layer, sprinkle a little of the herbs and seasoning. Try to finish with a layer of potatoes.

Pour the stock into the dish and add the Guinness.

In order to achieve the crispy potato topping, place a buttered greaseproof paper sheet on top of the casserole. Then place in the oven and cook for around two to two and a half hours.

This dish should serve four people and traditionally would be served with pickled red cabbage or buttered carrots.
Torn crusty bread is a must!

A TASTE OF
America

THE Cunard Yanks were the likely lads who helped forge Liverpool's cultural links with New York.

In the 1950s they brought a sense of New York glamour from their voyages across the Atlantic. When the Cunard ships docked at port after a 17-day voyage, our sailors would come ashore laden with treasures they had brought home - chocolates, electric guitars, refrigerators, records, beautiful clothes, new haircuts, new ideas. Some even claim the Cunard boys were responsible for a music revolution that influenced rock and roll - as well as four lads who shook the world.

Epic fayre at the Bar and Grill

The Renshaw Bar and Grill in Liverpool city centre offers the best of US dining – authentic American-style booths, friendly service, generous portions and delicious hearty American fayre. Resident chef Anthony Ungi has produced an eclectic menu which varies from healthy salads and light appetisers to barbecue ribs, mixed grill and traditional burgers, all of suitably epic proportions.

CLASSIC AMERICAN BURGER

Serves 4
450g lean mince beef, 1 small white onion very finely chopped, 2 tbsp sun dried tomato paste, 4 tbsp chopped fresh parsley, 1 large garlic clove crushed, 1 tsp mustard

For the topping
100g stilton cheese cut into chunks, 50g cherry tomatoes cut into halves

Combine the burger ingredients and season. Mould into four balls, and, with wet hands, shape into burgers about 3cm thick.

Cook the burgers for about 5 minutes each side, turning only once. Place onto a tray and put the stilton on top. Put under a grill until the cheese is melted and then put the burger into a bun with some rocket leaves, sprinkle the tomatoes over the top and serve with chunky chips.

Super-pie-banana
BANOFFEE PIE

The first shipment of bananas from the Canaries docked in England in 1882, while the American trade from Hawaii had been going for 20 years by that time. It was not until the great step of refrigerated ships that they arrived in London in 1901. For over a century, bananas were one of the major imports in Liverpool. Back then the banana was exotic and a luxury – now we just take them for granted.

Cooking bananas brings out their full flavour and they make a delicious dessert. Here, Anthony Ungi, resident chef at The Renshaw Bar and Grill, offers his recipe for banoffee pie.

Serves 4
Pie base
100g butter
250g digestive biscuits, crushed

For the caramel
175g butter
75g caster sugar
397g can condensed milk

For the topping
4 bananas, depending on size
320ml double cream, lightly whipped
Crushed almond flakes

8" loose bottomed cake tin greased and lined with baking paper

Crush the biscuit into fine crumbs with a rolling pin or use a blender. Next melt the butter and stir in the crushed biscuits until the two bind together. Press down into the base of a lined cake tin. Chill for 20 minutes in the fridge.

For the caramel, melt the butter and sugar over a low heat until the sugar has dissolved and the mixture is golden in colour. Add the condensed milk, stirring continuously and bring to the boil. Keep the caramel boiling steadily for 2 minutes whilst stirring. Take off the heat and allow to cool. When the caramel is cooled pour over the biscuit base and refrigerate for 1 hour.

When chilled slice the bananas and arrange them over the caramel. Fill a piping bag with whipped cream and squeeze onto the top of the banoffee pie. Spread the almond flakes on top and serve.

Lenny's rolls back the years

PULLED PORK WITH CRISPY ONIONS & BBQ BEANS

Inspired by legendary Chicago bars such as Bourbon & Branch and Please Don't Tell, Lenny's on Sir Thomas Street in Liverpool city centre, offers a flavour of the glamour, romance and secrecy of the 1920s prohibition era.

Head chef John Macloughlin is passionate about the food of America, relishing the contrast between the fine dining rooms of New York to the more rustic flavours of Tennessee. He spent a lot of time in the US researching many of the dishes for Lenny's and has come up with a menu which offers a truly authentic taste of 1920s prohibition America.

Serves 4

Pulled Pork
4 pork shoulder steaks
25g chopped lemon thyme
2 cloves of sliced garlic
3 tbsp of barbecue marinade
1 tbsp of lemon zest
3 tbsp of chopped onions
500ml chicken stock
4 cups of boiled, white long-grain rice

BBQ Beans
1 onion diced
1 green pepper diced
2 garlic cloves pureed
1 can of red beans
1 can of pinto beans
1 can of tomatoes
1 tbsp of tomato ketchup
1 tsp of chilli powder
1 tsp of black pepper
1 tsp mustard
1 tsp of hot sauce
1 cup of barbecue sauce

Crispy Onions
1 finely sliced onion
Half a cup of seasoned flour
Half a cup of milk

Pulled Pork

Marinade the pork in the barbecue marinade overnight, then seal the meat in a hot pan and remove to an ovenproof dish. Add the onions to the pan and cook for 2 minutes. Then add the thyme, garlic, lemon zest and chicken stock and bring to the boil. Put these ingredients over the pork in the dish. Cover with foil and cook for 90 minutes at 180°C until soft.

When cooked, remove the pork from the liquid and flake with a fork. Pass the stock through a sieve and reserve. Put the rice in one half of a deep bowl and the beans in another (see below for beans recipe). Place the pork on top and pour over a little of the reserved stock. Top with crispy onions (see below for recipe) and chopped parsley

BBQ Beans

Fry the onion and then add the peppers, garlic, chilli powder and mustard, and stir. Next add the tinned tomatoes, ketchup, hot sauce and barbecue sauce, and simmer for 20 minutes. Finally add the beans and simmer for 10 minutes.

Crispy Onions

Dip the onions in the milk and then the flour and deep fry until golden brown at 170°C.

Tradition with a twist
LUXURY HAM AND EGGS

Chef John Macloughlin, of Lenny's Bar & Smoke Grill, has taken this traditional American dish and given it a twist. Instead of using ham, he prefers to use slow roasted pork belly which helps to give the dish added flavour.

Serves 2
Slow roasted pork belly
500ml chicken stock
1kg belly pork, fat scored with a sharp knife
1 tbsp sea salt
1 tbsp fresh thyme leaves
2 toasted muffin circles in hot butter
2 poached eggs

Hollandaise sauce
3 tbsp of white wine vinegar
6 peppercorns
1 dried bay leaf
2 eggs, yolks only
125g butter
Lemon juice, salt and pepper to taste

Pork belly
Preheat the oven to 170°C/Gas 3. For the pork belly, pour boiling water over the pork skin and pat dry using kitchen paper. Then rub the salt and thyme leaves over the skin, pressing them into the score marks.

Seal in a hot pan and then cover with chicken stock and tin foil and cook for 2 hours. Remove the foil for the last 30 minutes to crisp up. Cool then slice into thin pieces. To reheat, seal in a hot skillet on both sides for 30 seconds, then place on top of the muffin, add the hot poached egg and top with hollandaise sauce and chopped parsley.

Hollandaise sauce
Put the vinegar in a small pan with the peppercorns and bay leaf. Reduce the vinegar over a high heat until there is only about 1 tablespoon left. Strain the peppercorns and the bay leaf from this reduction.

Put the egg yolks in a food processor with the vinegar reduction. Gently melt the butter so that the butter solids fall to the bottom of the saucepan.

Turn the food processor on and slowly pour the butter on to the egg yolks with the motor still running. The sauce will start to thicken. When only the butter solids are left, stop. If the sauce is too thick, add a little hot water. Season to taste with salt and pepper and a little lemon juice.

V Café breaks the mould

S'MORES BOARD

Offering an array of international cuisine, the V Café based at the Vincent Hotel in Southport, prides itself on being different from a traditional hotel restaurant. Head chef Martin Quinlan has one very popular signature dish; the S'mores board dessert – marshmallows, caramel, chocolate dips and cinnamon biscuits, all toasted on a flame at the table and finished with ice cream!

Martin said: "S'mores board is extremely popular in the US, which was where we first came across the recipe, and we're probably the first place in the North West to bring the American treat to Britain. "We only recently introduced the American pudding to the dessert list and it's already flying off the menu. People love being able to toast their own marshmallows over the flame, it certainly adds a bit of theatre to the table."

Serves 6
Marshmallows
A pot of caramel sauce
A pot of chocolate sauce
Ice cream

To make the cinnamon biscuits:
100g self raising flour
150g plain flour
2 tsp ground cinnamon
125g butter
100g sugar
1 egg beaten

Preheat oven to 160°C and beat the butter, sugar and egg into a large bowl, then sift in the flour and the cinnamon and mix together. Roll out the mixture on a board using a rolling pin and then use a cutter to cut into your desired shape. Bake in the oven for 10-15 minutes until golden. Place the cinnamon biscuits, marshmallows and caramel and chocolate dips on a plate with two skewers and a pot of non-toxic chafing gel fuel – this can be be bought at catering or camping shops. Soak the skewers in water first before placing them on the plate. To finish your dessert off perfectly, add your favourite ice cream to the side.

Toast your marshmallow over the flame until golden brown, slip it off the skewer and place between the two cinnamon biscuits. Dip into the chocolate and caramel sauce and add a touch of ice cream on top.

How to toast the perfect marshmallow
1.Loading the marshmallow
To load the marshmallow place it far enough onto the skewer that it does not fall off into the fire once it gets hot. However, don't push it too far or you may find it difficult to remove.

2.Cooking the marshmallow
For a perfectly-toasted marshmallow, briskly move the skewer over the top of the flames until it is golden brown. This will make it slightly crispy on the outside and gooey on the inside. Do not stick it directly into the fire as this will blacken and burn the marshmallow.

3.Removing the marshmallow
Remove the marshmallow from the flame and allow it to cool for about 20-30 seconds. Hold the skewer with one hand and slowly pull the whole marshmallow off with the other hand. Get a friend to help you by sandwiching the marshmallow between the cinnamon biscuits and pulling it off the skewer.

ALMA DE CUBA: A RELIGION

HISTORICALLY Cuba has been influenced by a variety of cultures. Reflecting this, Alma de Cuba's menu features flavours and spices from around the world - particularly the Caribbean, Spain and Latin America.

Set inside the former St Peter's Catholic Church complete with original altar and stained glass windows; the Seel Street restaurant makes for an atmospheric place to eat - and work - as it was the restaurant's unusual church setting which first attracted head chef, Jamie Robertson, to Liverpool.

A flair for flavour

SLOW ROASTED JERK CHICKEN WITH SCALLION AND THYME GRAVY

Serves 4
For the marinade
4 chicken thigh bones
4 chicken drumsticks
5 dessert spoons of hot jerk paste

For the scallion and thyme gravy
1 small onion
1 litre rich dark chicken jus
10g fresh thyme
Salt to taste
Fresh milled pepper to taste

For the coconut rice 'n' peas
250g basmati rice
2 litres water
400g red kidney beans
400g tin coconut milk (authentic Thai as this has a richer cream content)
3 spring onions
2 dessert spoons fresh thyme
Salt and black pepper
1 clove of fresh garlic, peeled and finely crushed

To serve
2 spring onions
1 medium hot red chilli
8 sprigs of fresh coriander

Here is Jamie Robertson's recipe for an Alma de Cuba favourite . . .

Score the chicken through the skin and flesh to the bone. Place all the marinade ingredients into a mixing bowl and work the jerk paste into each piece of scored chicken. Marinade for a minimum of 12 hours but no more than 48 hours (depending upon how hot you want the flavour). Keep the chicken in the fridge until needed.

Heat the sauté pan over a moderate heat. Seal the chicken pieces on all sides, cook for approximately three minutes per side then place into a colander over a draining tray. Ensure that the onion is very finely diced, add a splash of oil, then add the onion to the pan and sweat down for approximately five to eight minutes until soft and tender with a little caramelisation.

Whilst the onion is cooking, place the rich dark jus into a saucepan and bring to the boil. Add the chopped thyme leaves to the sweated onion and stir in. Add the simmered rich chicken jus and bring back to the boil. Place the chicken pieces into a casserole dish with the skin side facing up, then pour over the hot onion jus. Place into a moderate oven approximately 140°C and cook for approximately 90 minutes or until very tender – but not falling off the bone. Once cooked, if not serving straight away, chill as quickly as possible, place into a suitable container and refrigerate until needed.

To make the coconut rice 'n' peas, place twice as much water into a pan as the quantity of dry rice. Lightly salt the water and bring to the boil. Add the pre-rinsed rice and cook until al dente – do not over cook.

Once the rice is cooked, refresh under cold running water then drain well. Put the drained rice into a mixing bowl, add the kidney beans, trimmed and sliced spring onions, fresh thyme and garlic and mix together thoroughly. Stir in the coconut cream, taste and season accordingly. Place into a suitable container and refrigerate until needed.

Place the slow roasted chicken and gravy into a suitable pan and reheat thoroughly – this must reach above 78°C. Check that the chicken pieces are piping hot all the way to the bone. Slice the red chilli into very thin rings and cook for ten minutes.

Place the rice 'n' peas into a suitable dish and microwave until heated through thoroughly. Check that the rice is piping hot before serving. Add the finely shredded spring onion and cooked chilli rings to the slow roasted chicken. Serve immediately and garnish with the fresh coriander.

Friendly fire

POLLO COCO

Serves 4

For the chicken marinade
5 chicken breasts diced
150ml palm oil
4 chipotle chillies in adobo sauce
4 tbsp fresh coriander
2 tbsp crushed garlic
1 tbsp ginger, 1 tbsp smoked paprika
1 tbsp chilli powder, 1 tbsp oregano
Salt and pepper

For the coconut sauce
1 large onion
2 tins coconut milk
2 tbsp crushed garlic, fresh coriander

For the salsa
Chopped tomatoes, 3 shallots
1 chipotle chilli, 1 red capsicum
4 roasted garlic cloves (crushed)
1 fresh jalapeno pepper
Fresh chopped coriander

Chris Hamblin, head chef at Savina Mexican Restaurant and Cantina, was given these recipes by a family friend from Santa Cruz del Valle in Guadalajara. For authenticity, the Duke Street cantina has all of its chillies imported by a Mexican goods supplier.

To give the chicken a smokey flavour in Savina's Pollo Coco dish, Chris, who started his culinary career 16 years ago, uses chipotle chilli – a smoked jalapeno pepper which he buys in adobo sauce. Use Mexican oregano if possible.

Mix all of the marinade ingredients, add the chicken breasts and leave over night. To make the chicken, fry one large onion until golden brown then add the marinated chicken. Cook until golden brown and leave to one side.

Now cook the coconut sauce. Fry the diced onion and the garlic until golden brown, add the coconut milk and bring to boil. Blend and leave to cool. When the coconut sauce is cool, add the fresh chopped coriander. To prepare the salsa, add of all the ingredients, finely chopped, in a mixing bowl and combine.

To finish the dish add the coconut milk and salsa to the chicken and simmer for 10-15 minutes. Dress the dish with caramelised red onion and chipotle chillies.

Savina knows its chillies

Chillies are essential to Mexican cookery, but to ensure you add the right flavour – not just heat – you need to use the right types. For the Zarzuela dish, Chris Hamblin uses ancho chilli for a sweet but mildly spicey taste. You can buy chipotle, ancho and guajilo chillies, as well as achiote seeds, via Savina on Duke Street.

ZARZUELA DE PESCADOS

Serves 4

4 garlic cloves (thinly sliced), 2 tsp of palm oil, 1 onion (thinly sliced) 150ml white wine, 1 tbsp fresh sliced ginger, 150ml fresh fish stock 1 tin chopped tomatoes, 1 tsp cumin, 1 tsp hot paprika, 1 tsp Chili Piquin Pepper 2 dried ancho chillies (soak the ancho chilli overnight in salt water and puree in a food processor), Salt and pepper, 12 scallops, 12 greenlip mussels, 16 king prawns 8 bay leaves

Add the oil to the pan and fry the garlic and the onions until golden brown. Add the ginger and white wine, reduce by half then add the fish stock and chopped tomatoes. Next, add ancho chillies and the rest of the ingredients. Simmer for around 15-20 minutes, adding more stock if needed, then add the fish of your choice. Serve with fresh crusty bread.

Learn Latin in Liverpool

CHURRASCO STEAK

Originally from Gran Canaria, Spain, MEET Argentinian Restaurant's head chef, Juan Manuel Hidalgo, has learnt more about Latin food in Liverpool than anywhere else.

The 36-year-old's first full time chef's job was in a Gran Canarian restaurant owned by an Argentinian couple. "It was hard work but when I look back, it was worth it because they taught me a lot about South American cuisine," says Juan.

Juan's next role was in a more upmarket Argentinian steakhouse where he learnt about refined South American cuisine. And, since moving to Liverpool, the passionate LFC fan, who has 19 years' experience, has worked for several hotels, gastro pubs and restaurants, including Don Pepe Spanish restaurant on Victoria Street, the former MEET Brazilian restaurant and MEET Argentinian on Brunswick Street, where he has been head chef for almost five years.

Serves 2
16oz-20oz prime sirloin steak

For the Alinado Marinade
2 large onions
2 bulbs of fresh garlic
1 glass of white wine
1 tbsp English mustard
A pinch of black pepper
1 tsp table salt
150ml olive oil

For the chimichurri sauce
1 bunch fresh oregano
1 bunch fresh parsley
1 bunch fresh coriander
6 bulbs of garlic
12 spring onions
2 white onions
8 tomatoes
6 bell peppers
Sea salt, to taste
Half a teaspoon of black pepper
1 tsp chilli flakes
2 tbsp paprika
100ml olive oil
300ml red wine vinegar

First, trim any fat off the sirloin steak and put aside while you prepare a marinade called alinado. To make the alinado marinade, roughly chop the onions and garlic, place in a food processor or blender with the wine, salt, pepper, mustard and a little bit of oil, start blending and, after 30 seconds, start adding a little bit of oil at a time until it's all gone.

Now, dip your trimmed sirloin into the marinade and put in the fridge for at least three to four hours (the longer the better).

While the meat is marinating, make the chimichurri sauce by blitzing all ingredients together in a food processor or blender until you get a pesto-like consistency. Check the seasoning and adjust to your own taste.

Lastly, take the sirloin steak out of the fridge and leave to rest for a few minutes before you cook it. Ideally the best way to cook the steak is on a charcoal grill, but you could pan-fry or grill it. Take the meat out of the alinado marinade and cook on a chargrill, grill or frying pan until it's almost done to your liking.

At this point, let the meat rest for five minutes and then slice into thick slabs at a 45 degree angle. Transfer the sliced steak to a clean frying pan or tray, cover with the chimichurri sauce and place under the grill or in the oven for a just a couple of minutes to finish. Serve the sliced steak with tomato, bacon and salad.

Labour of love

HOMEMADE BBQ RIBS

Serves 2
1.8kg baby back pork ribs
500g brown sugar
4tbsp Worcester sauce
100ml soy sauce
100g tomato paste

For the chimichurri marinade:
1 bunch fresh oregano
1 bunch fresh parsley
1 bunch fresh coriander
6 bulbs of garlic
12 spring onions
2 white onions
8 tomatoes
6 bell peppers
sea salt, to taste
0.5 tsp black pepper
1 tsp chilli flakes
2 tbsp paprika
1 litre olive oil
300ml red wine vinegar

MEET Argentinian's head chef, Juan Manuel Hidalgo, says: "Here is where I've learned the most about Latin food as I've had the chance to work with loads of people from all over South America including Argentina, Colombia, Brazil, Peru, Ecuador, Chile, Bolivia and even Cuba.

"I've been here for nearly 14 years and I'm still in love with cooking and the city."

Wash the ribs and pat dry with kitchen towel. Next you need to prepare the chimichurri marinade. Chimichurri is a traditional Argentinian sauce which is very easy to make. Blend all of the marinade ingredients – except for the brown sugar, soy sauce, Worcester sauce, tomato paste and sea salt – together in a food processor or blender. It should have a similar consistency to pesto.

Now dip your racks of ribs one-by-one in the marinade and put into a deep baking tray, making sure the ribs are covered by the marinade. Cover with foil and cook in a oven at 130°C for three hours. If you're not using a fan-assisted oven, make sure that you turn the tray around every half hour.

For the final stage, drain the cooked marinade into a pan, heat gently and skim the fat off the surface. Add the brown sugar, soy sauce, tomato paste, Worcester sauce and salt to taste and bring to the boil, reduce until you get a syrup like sauce.

Take the sauce off the heat, pour onto the ribs and put them back in the oven for a further 35-45 minutes uncovered at 190°C, making sure you baste the ribs with the marinade when starting to burn inside the oven.

Pele's favourite
XINXIM

Xinxim is a Brazilian lime chicken dish in a creamy crayfish and peanut sauce served with rice, fine green beans and coconut farofa (toasted manioc flour) to sprinkle over for added crunch and sweet plantain. Said to be Pele's favourite dish, Xinxim is an example of the fusion between Portuguese, African and native Latin American Indian cuisines.

At Las Iguanas in Liverpool ONE, Xinxim is served in terracotta burners made especially for Las Iguanas in Brazil.

Serves 6
6 chicken breasts, skinless & boneless
100g crayfish tails
1 small diced onion
1 clove fresh garlic
30g butter
1 level tbsp chilli puree
50ml lemon juice
25ml lime juice
350ml whipping cream
100ml water
1 fish stock cube
227g peanut butter
Salt and black pepper
3 level tbsp unrefined palm oil

Place the butter and palm oil into a large flat casserole or roasting tray on a medium hob. Gently fry the chicken breasts to colour all over then remove from the tray.

Add the onion, garlic and chilli puree to the tray and fry without colouring, then crumble in the fish stock cube and stir in. Add the lemon and lime juices, whipping cream, water and peanut butter, and stir together.

Put the chicken back in (you can cut it into strips if you wish or keep it as whole pieces), add the crayfish, cover and place in an oven at 220°C to braise for approximately 1 hour. When ready, the sauce should have slightly thickened.

Serve with white rice, fine green beans and a garnish of watercress. Additional accompaniments include fried plantain and coconut farofa.

Street eat

PORK BURRITOS

Fast, fresh, fiery and packed with flavour, street food is a big part of Mexican culture, where typical street fayre includes the likes of quesadillas, tacos and burritos which can be eaten on-the-go.

Inspired by authentic Mexican street stalls, Barburrito offers classic burritos with a western twist. For authenticity, Barburrito sources its Mexican ingredients from importers. If you're looking to buy the specialist ingredients required for this dish, like Mexican oregano and achiote seeds, the restaurant recommends using the website www.coolchile.co.uk

Serves 8

2 tbsp achiote seeds
2 tsp allspice, freshly ground
1 tsp black pepper, freshly ground
One and a half teaspoons of dried Mexican oregano
3 tbsp cider vinegar
6 garlic cloves, minced
1 generous tsp salt
6 tbsp Seville orange juice
900g lean, boneless pork shoulder
200g white rice
200g pinto beans
14-16 tortilla wraps
Tobasco sauce
Romaine lettuce, chopped
Sour cream
Tomato and onion salsa
Guacamole

First make the achiote seasoning paste. Pulverise the achiote seeds in a spice grinder then transfer to a small bowl and add allspice, pepper, Mexican oregano and vinegar. Combine to make a crumbly, thick mixture. Roughly chop the garlic, sprinkle with salt, and work into a smooth paste with the side of your knife. Add the achiote mixture and work the two together, then add enough water – about one to two tablespoons – to make a thick, spreadable paste.

In a large bowl, mix the achiote seasoning and juice together. Add the pork, coat evenly, cover and leave to marinate in the fridge for at least two hours.

Turn the oven to 160°C and place the pork into a large, oven-proof pot, drizzle 250ml water around the meat, cover tightly and oven roast for about three hours, until the meat is very tender and falls apart. Whilst the meat is roasting, occasionally check how much water is in the pot, adding more if it has evaporated.

Once cooked, place the pork onto a cutting board, pour the juices from the pan into a large jug and let both cool slightly. Spoon the fat off the juices, roughly chop or shred the meat, sprinkle with a little salt and return to the pot. Pour a small amount of the juice onto the pork to keep it moist. Cover the pork and keep warm over a low heat.

Cook the rice according to the pack's instructions. Whilst the rice is cooking, simmer the pinto beans in a pan with plenty of room for stirring – keep the heat low and stir often to keep the beans from burning.

To make each individual burrito, warm a 12-inch tortilla wrap in a dry frying pan until it softens. Add a large spoonful of cooked rice to the tortilla, followed by a spoonful of pinto beans. Next add the chopped or shredded pork, some tomato and onion salsa, fresh guacamole and Tobasco or chili sauce to spice it up to your taste.

Top with a sprinkle of chopped romaine lettuce and finish with sour cream. Pinch both ends to form a burrito and serve.

Sunshine food
JERK CHICKEN

When you think of the Caribbean, you think of sea, sunshine, white sands and, of course, fabulous food.

And Nigerian-born Grace Adegoke, who runs RNK Caterers and Cookery School, has brought those fantastic flavours and a taste of sunshine to Wirral. Grace specialises in offering a fusion of modern and traditional Afro-Caribbean cuisine, with a big focus on making the food as healthy as possible.

"There is a very laid back approach to cooking in Africa and the Caribbean, they cook three meals a day and cooking is part of the lifestyle in this part of the world, it is not seen as a chore. "Everybody chips in with the cooking – they put everything in together and 'jerk' it up."

Many of the ingredients used in Grace's food can be purchased from her website www.rnk-foods.co.uk. Her own recipe book, entitled 'Cooking is Fun – Afro-Caribbean Style' is out now. "It is very easy to cook Afro-Caribbean food once you know the ingredients," says Grace.

Serves 3-4
6 chicken fillets (or chicken on the bone)
1 tsp ground allspice
1 tsp thyme
2 garlic cloves, crushed
1 small onion, chopped
A quarter cup of chopped spring onions
2 tbsp grated ginger
Half tbsp vinegar
2 tbsp vegetable oil
A squeeze of lime or lemon juice
2 tsp brown sugar (optional)
Scotch bonnet pepper or chilli to taste, chopped
Salt and ground black pepper to taste

Combine all the ingredients in a bowl to form a thick paste. Make lengthways slits in the chicken. Rub the marinade all over the chicken and into the slits.

Cover with clear film and marinate in the fridge overnight or for some hours. Remove any excess marinade before cooking.

Brush the chicken with oil and place on the grill, BBQ or in the oven. Cook for about 20-30 mins, turning at intervals (cook for longer if on the bone).
Serve with rice and peas, or salad.

Celebrating African music and culture at Africa Oyé in Sefton Park

Brian Wong,
owner of
the Hondo
supermarket

Chinatown

LIVERPOOL'S Chinatown - the oldest in Europe - is centred around Nelson Street, where the magnificent Chinese Arch stands as a 'symbol of hope'.

But the original Chinatown sprang up closer to the river - in Cleveland Square, near the south end of Paradise Street. The first wave of Chinese immigrants arrived in 1866 following the establishment of the Blue Funnel Shipping Line, a branch of the Holt Ocean Steamship Company, which ran a line of steamers directly from Liverpool to China. The quiet, shy Chinese, kept themselves to themselves and dined on the supplies of food they had brought from home.

Soon, enterprising residents opened shops selling whatever was brought over on the ships, like Mr Kwong's Kwongsang Lung Grocery Store, on Pitt Street, one of seven by 1906.

Businessman Brian Wong owns Chinese supermarket Hondo, which still sells food that would have been eaten at the time.

"It took three months to get it here, as they had to sail round Cape Horn, so everything was preserved or salted," he says.

"They would cut a couple of slices from salted fish and eat it with rice and a lot of soy or plum sauce. For vegetables, they would have pickled mustard greens, dried cole - pak choi boiled then dried in long strings - preserved turnip, which was steamed and served with beef, and they'd always bring dried Chinese mushrooms."

Protein also came via sticks of dried beancurd and thousand-year eggs - duck eggs 'cured' for 100 days in a clay-like mixture of strong tea, ashes, lime and salt, and eaten in slices with sweet pickled vegetables.

"They are dishes that are still enjoyed today," says Brian, who also organises Liverpool's Chinese New Year celebrations. "Salted fish or fried dace (mud carp) in a container with a bit of ginger and eaten with a bit of rice. Delicious."

By the 1980s, Peking restaurants had emerged, alongside the old-style Cantonese. Most now boast a mix of styles from different regions, each of which is fond of a specific flavour.

"In Sechuan province, the mid-west and the interior, where the weather is hot and humid, they like hot, spicy food," says Brian. "Whereas, in Peking and Shanghai, they like sour, pickled tastes in dishes. The Cantonese in the south, like Hong Kong, prefer salty and sweet."

Ching-He Huang

THE CAPITAL OF SUI MAI

SCOUSE might be the traditional native dish of Liverpudlians, but one man is making it his mission to put a Far East staple at the forefront of the city's cuisine map.

Perry Ng, managing director of Golden Dragon Food, says that Liverpool has become the capital of sui mai, with more sold on Merseyside than anywhere else in Britain.

"Everybody in Liverpool has heard of sui mai – people might say that Scouse is the city's favourite dish, but if I stood on the street and asked passers-by which they ate more of, the answer would be sui mai," says Perry, who produces the delicious Chinese dumplings from his factory in Jamaica Street.

As well as proving a big hit with supermarkets, takeaways and restaurants in Merseyside, Golden Dragon's sui mais are exported all over the UK and even Europe.

"My father came to Liverpool in the 1960s because he loved the Beatles," says Perry.

"He set up his own company importing food from the Far East and distributing it all over the UK. When I left school I went to work for him – he taught me everything I know.

"The tradition behind sui mai was using up leftover meat, which was sliced up and then used inside the dumplings - so it's quite similar to Scouse in that respect.

"I always tell my chefs to open their eyes, be open to new ideas and create something new every week. We've been experimenting with some new sui mai flavours which are proving really popular."

Celebrity chefs Ian Pengelley and Ching-He Huang have been spotted on the sui mai trail, visiting Perry's Buffet Club restaurant on Prescot Street, in a bid to discover why Scouse sui mais are number one.

Ching, presenter of BBC television's Chinese Food Made Easy, says: "I love the classic pork sui mai using delicious seasoned pork and dried Chinese mushrooms. It's one of my favourite dim sum dishes. So when I was invited to The Buffet Club to try some new and unique sui mai dishes such as Rendang, Tom Yum and Szechuan, I just couldn't resist."

The Buffet Club has already established itself as a firm favourite in the city, serving five-star food at affordable prices. So, what next for Liverpool's sui mai king?

"In Singapore and Hong Kong, sui mai is sold in supermarkets and corner shops in these huge steaming machines. You can buy it as a snack on a stick, like a hot dog! I want to take sui mai to the next level - it's going to be the next big thing, bigger than sushi and bigger than Scouse!"

Perry Ng (left)
Liverpool's Sui Mai king

www.buffetclub.co.uk

A Chinese institution

KWO-TA CHICKEN

One of Liverpool's oldest and most revered Chinese restaurants, the institution that is the Yuet Ben has more excellent reviews and customer testimonials than you can shake a spare rib at.

Yuet Ben – whose name means 'honoured guest' – originally stood on Great George Street. The restaurant was opened in 1968 by Shandong-born Yuh Ho Yau, who learnt his culinary skills in Dalian and worked in restaurants in Hong Kong, Beijing and New York before settling in Liverpool. These days Yuet Ben is run by Yuh's daughter Theresa and her husband who make it their mission to bring to Liverpool authentic tastes and flavours of Northern China.

Yuet Ben is what Chinese food should be all about. The venue itself is far from fancy but you don't need shiny lights and designer furniture when your food is this good and such great value, plus choose the right table and you will get a fabulous view of the Chinese Arch.

Here, the renowned restaurant shares its recipe for Kwo-ta chicken.

Serves 2

One large chicken breast (skinned and de-boned)
Corn flour or plain flour
2 eggs, beaten
4 tbsp oil for frying
4 tbsp chicken stock
2 tbsp rice wine or sherry
2 cloves garlic
1 spring onion
Piece of shredded ginger
Half tsp sugar
Quarter tsp salt

Slice the chicken into three or four pieces, coat them in flour before dipping them in a bowl of beaten egg. Heat the oil in a wok or frying pan and then fry the coated slices of chicken on both sides. Once cooked, remove and cut them up into bite-size pieces before placing on a serving dish.

Prepare the sauce with stock and wine. Add in the sliced garlic, spring onion (cut into inch long pieces), shredded ginger, sugar and salt. Bring to boil and finally pour over the chicken.

Serve with plain boiled rice so that the fragrance of the garlic, spring onion, ginger and wine sauce can be savoured and not masked by a stronger flavoured complement.

Thai's hotter than ever

IT'S healthy, light, packed with flavour and reassuringly exotic. Demand for good Thai food is hot on Merseyside, with Thai restaurants never as ubiquitous as their high street Chinese counterparts.

And with Thai food now widely available, people want to try their hand at dishes from South East Asia that are healthy and authentic.

Chef Thanyanan Phuaknapo - nicknamed Pum - runs Thai cookery workshops at Chaophraya in Liverpool and Manchester.

"Thai food has got more popular and people want to know how to cook it at home," she explains.

Green or red curry paste should be store cupboard staples, says Pum. She recommends Nittaya brand.

While the fresh pastes are excellent, pounding the herbs and spices yourself is more authentically Thai.

"You can use paste but in Thailand we like to pound the ingredients together with a pestle and mortar," says Pum. "It should take about an hour.

"You cover the bowl with your hand and just bang the ingredients. You don't get the essential oil out of the skin so well using a blender."

Kang Pa, jungle curry, is less of a menu staple than green or red, but just as tasty. It isn't mixed with coconut milk. The end result is sweet and hot.

Pum says: "In history, it was what you used in the jungle when you were hot and needed something hotter to eat. You wouldn't have had coconut milk but you would cut some vegetables and kill an animal. You put what you found into the pot, with water and some sugar cane."

Tom Yam - meaning clear soup - is another favourite. The paste is available in supermarkets, but making your own is easy.

"The stock is made from boiling a chicken bone in water, nothing more than that," says Pum. "Add any chicken or prawns you have, put in the lemon grass, lime leaf, chilli and galangal, leave that to boil. Then you season with fish sauce and a little bit of sugar." She suggests adding any "non-juicy" vegetable, like cauliflower.

Dishes vary enormously across Thailand, according to local ingredients. In the North, away from the sea, spicy pork or beef sausage tend to be very popular. Very hot dishes tend to come from Southern Thailand, often seafood-based.

"If you have the ingredients, Thai food is simple to prepare, healthy and very tasty."

Wind your way to Chaophraya

TOM YUM KOONG

Named after the main waterway flowing through Thailand, Chaophraya brings fine Thai dining to Liverpool in a luxurious setting with award-winning cuisine.

Owner Kim Atcharaporn Kaewkraikhot had a dream to bring the essence of Thailand to England and enlisted only the finest Thai chefs and staff to open the first Chaophraya restaurant, pronounced chow-pie-a, in 2004.

The chefs chose one of the region's most popular dishes, the hot and spicy prawn soup 'Tom Yum Koong', authentic Thai cuisine. The recipe is said to have first been recorded in Thailand in 1889, although it never included galangal at this time, instead using tamarind.

Serves 4-6

15 tiger prawns or shrimps
100g mushrooms
600g chicken stock
1 tbsp chopped lemongrass
1 tbsp chopped galangal
3-4 kaffir lime leaves
3-4 chillies
5 tbsp fish sauce
4 tbsp lime juice
1 tbsp chili oil
1 tbsp chopped coriander

Clean the prawns and remove the black thread (the intestine) by cutting it down the back. Slice the galangal and lemongrass into short 3cm pieces and pound them in a mortar to break out the flavours. Put the chicken stock in a pan and bring to the boil. When the water is boiling add the galangal, lemongrass, kaffir lime leaves, salt, and wait for it to boil again. Add the shrimps and cook for two minutes.

Break the chillies into a mortar and pound them for a few moments to a pulp, and add to the soup. Add the sliced mushrooms, fish sauce, lime juice and chilli oil to the soup. Turn off the heat and add the coriander leaves, serve hot.

View to Matou

MALAYSIAN CHICKEN CURRY

Set overlooking Liverpool's world-famous waterfront, Matou delivers big pan-Asian flavours, cooking everything fresh to achieve the best taste. Head chef Payung is from Thailand, and an expert in creating authentic dishes using traditional ingredients adapted to British palates.

"We get a lot of our ingredients from local Asian supermarkets where the products are brought in from Thailand such as lemongrass, but all our meat is sourced locally to ensure it's fresh," says joint owner Danny Boon.

"I chose this recipe as I've always cooked it at home and my children love it, the flavours are delicious, so when we opened Matou, early 2010, it was one of the dishes we decided to put on the menu."

Serves 4
Whole fresh chicken
Peeled potatoes

For the Curry Paste
5 shallots
2" stem lemongrass
2" stem ginger
2" stem galangal
Fresh coriander
1 whole onion
Salt and sugar to taste
500ml of water
Cup of coconut milk
3 whole dried red chillies
Curry leaves

Cut up the chicken into pieces, leaving in the bones. Put the shallots, lemongrass, galangal, ginger, coriander and onion into a blender and mix to a coarse paste. Then chop the potatoes.

Heat a deep pan and add oil, saute the blended ingredients until aromatic or light brown in colour. Add the curry paste to the pan and stir until aromatic. Then add the chicken pieces, stir until they are sealed, then add in the water.

Cover the pan with the lid and bring the curry chicken to the boil. Add the potatoes and then lower the heat and let the curry simmer for 30 minutes until the chicken is tender. Add the coconut milk and bring to the boil, then add salt and sugar to taste. Garnish with a sprig of coriander, stem of lemongrass, dried red chili and curry leaves, serve hot with steamed rice.

Aussie influence

TIGER PRAWN AND PINEAPPLE SKEWERS WITH A BLACK PEPPER GLAZE

Ashley Richey, head chef at HOST, Hope Street's great pan-Asian restaurant, loves to include his influence from Down Under when putting together the exciting menus.

Ashley, originally from Australia, worked in Sydney for a number of years before moving over to the UK to take up the head chef position at HOST. And we all know how they like a 'barbie' Down Under!

"This is a great, simple, but flavour packed barbecue recipe that will tantalise your taste buds. Your fishmonger can do all of the dirty work for you and you can even make a larger batch of the black pepper glaze and freeze it for up to a month to use at the next BBQ," says Ashley.

Try this delicious, quick and fun starter, with a black pepper glaze, which is easy to make, leaving plenty of time to relax and enjoy your meal!

Serves 4 as a starter
12 large uncooked tiger prawns, shelled
1 whole pineapple

For the Black Pepper Glaze
3 spring onions
1 tbsp ginger
2 cloves of garlic
1 tbsp crushed black pepper
1 tbsp blackbeans
50ml kecap manis (sweet soy sauce, available in supermarkets)
25ml light soy sauce
1 tbsp tamarind water
1tbsp caster sugar
1 tsp salt

For the Black Pepper Glaze
Finely chop the spring onions, ginger, and garlic, sauté in a little vegetable oil, then add the black pepper and rinsed black beans and sauté for a further two minutes. Add the remaining ingredients and simmer for two minutes, then blend with a hand blender.

For the skewers
Cut the skin off the pineapple and cut into rectangular pieces, roughly the size and thickness of the prawns. Thread the shelled prawns and pineapple onto bamboo skewers (roughly two/three prawns per skewer with pineapple threaded around each prawn).

Lightly oil the skewers and cook on the BBQ or under a grill until prawns are just done, this will take around two/three minutes. Brush with the warmed black pepper glaze before serving and enjoy.

Tip: If cooking the skewers on the BBQ, soak the bamboo skewers in water for 30 minutes beforehand to stop them from burning.

Sakura: A fresh approach

WATARIGANI MAKI

Bringing contemporary Japanese dining to Liverpool has been the vision driving the team at Sakura, in Liverpool's Exchange Flags, from day one.

"We have managed to find live seabass that we keep in tanks in the restaurant, right next to live lobsters and scallops," says head chef Girish Gopalakrishnan. "Let alone in the UK, not many restaurants in Europe can boast seafood this fresh."

Executive chef Masamitsu Morino, who has been at the forefront of Japanese cooking for the last 30 years, brings with him both classic and contemporary styles of Japanese dining.

"We go to great lengths to source seafood locally and only the best makes it to the plate," said Masamitsu.
This sushi-style recipe showcases the technical and culinary skills that make Sakura such an experience.

Serves 2
1 softshell crab
500g Japanese Katakuriko (Japanese violet flour)
120g Boiled Japanese round grain rice
20ml Sushi vinegar
4 tbsp mayonnaise and 1tbsp chilli paste (tobanjan) mixed together
1 sheet dried nori seaweed
Few roquette/rocket leaves
Soy
Wasabi paste
Gari (pickled ginger)
Tobiko (Flying fish roe)

For the crab
Heat the fryer to 180°C. Dust the whole crab in Katakuriko and fry until golden.(Caution has to be exercised while frying softshell crab as the oil may sputter. A lid would be appropriate).

To prepare the rice
Once the rice is cooked add the sushi vinegar in batches and 'cut' the rice with a wooden spatula taking care not to rupture the grain. Keep warm. (This ensures flavourful rice that holds together but falls apart when eaten).

Place a sushi mat on a clean surface. Push the rice onto a sheet of nori seaweed to form a thin layer about 6 mm thick. Then place the warm fried soft shell crab lengthways so the claws remain outside the rice and nori. Spread a small layer of the chilli mayonnaise and a few roquette/rocket leaves and roll the sheet away from you and seal the nori together with water thus forming a roll. Cut the roll across using a sharp knife into bite size slices.
Serve with tobiko, gari, soy and wasabi.

A drama at Sapporo
RAMEN NOODLE SOUP

Sapporo, one of Liverpool's first Japanese restaurants, shows us the true teppanyaki way with theatrical cooking demonstrations, along with freshly made cuisine and sushi.

In 2003 when the restaurant opened in Duke Street, Vudti Chai Taemsiri, affectionately known as Woody, became head chef after previously showcasing his skills at numerous restaurants across Asia.

Woody began life as a chef at the age of 19 and has a real passion for Asian cuisine, as well as Liverpool Football Club.

Serves 1
Half a litre of water
2 tbsp of soy sauce
1 tbsp of mirin wine
1 tsp of sesame oil
120g ramen noodles
30g pork loin (roasted or boiled according to your individual tastes)
30g Japanese/kamaboko fish cake (available to buy ready made from Asian supermarkets)
Half a boiled egg
1 spring onion
Grated/thinly sliced carrot
Handful of pak choi

Boil the water, soy sauce, mirin wine and sesame oil. When this comes to the boil, leave to simmer for five minutes, to create the soup base.

In the meantime, boil the ramen noodles in a separate pan of boiling water – this should only take a few minutes. Also lightly stir fry the pak choi and carrot in a little oil for two or three minutes.

Transfer the soup base and noodles into a bowl. Slice the pork and the fish cake then add them to the soup along with the boiled egg.

To serve, decorate with the spring onions, carrot and pak choi. Enjoy!

Etsu experience
TEMPURA

Hiroshi Ohara Tokuyama joined the team at Etsu in 2009 and has over 20 years of experience. "I chose the Tempura recipe as its quite commonly known here in the UK and its an easy dish to attempt at home yet still a large amount of skill is involved to produce quality Tempura," says Hiroshi.

Preparation
Put two egg yolks into a bowl of cold water and add in some ice cubes, then leave in fridge for 30 minutes.
Leaving the tails on, make an incision along the back of each prawn and take out the black thread. Then wash the prawns in cold water. Fillet the white fish taking out the bones and intestines, then wash in cold water. Put the fish and prawns onto a tray, sprinkling sake and salt over them. Grate the mooli and the ginger root separately. Make a small ball from the mooli and add a spot of ginger on top.

Serves 2
8 black tiger prawns (medium size headless/shelled)
2 small whole white fish
4 slices of potato
4 slices of pumpkin
4 slices of aubergine
4 pieces of shiitake mushroom
8 pieces of green pepper
200g mooli (Japanese white radish)
50g fresh ginger root
500g plain white flour
2 egg yolks
Handful of ice cubes
2 litres sunflower oil
300ml sesame oil
4 paper serviettes
275ml fish stock
75ml dark soy sauce
75ml mirin sake or rice wine

Method
Sift two thirds of the flour and then add to the bowl of egg yolks and water from the fridge, saving the rest of the flour for later. Gently mix the bowl ensuring the batter stays 'lumpy'. Cover the prawns, white fish and vegetables with the remaining flour. Shake off any excess flour and place into the batter mixture. Pour the sunflower and sesame oil into a big deep pot (deep fat fryer) and heat the oil to 170-180°C. Take the vegetables from the batter mixture, ensuring they are coated, and then gently slide them into the hot oil and deep fry until golden brown, turning occasionally.

Pinch the tail of the prawns and white fish and coat in batter, apart from the tails. Gently slide them into the oil and deep fry until golden brown. Remove and place onto a baking rack to drain any excess oil. Dish up the tempura onto plates lined with a paper serviette and place the mooli and ginger ball onto the side of the plate. Pour the fish stock, dark soy and mirin into a pan and heat until boiling, serving in small white dipping bowls. Add the mooli and ginger ball into the sauce. Dip the tempura and enjoy!

Mastering Japanese

MAGURO TATSUTA AGE (MARINATED FRIED TUNA)

Etsu's head chef, Tatsuya Ueda, was well known in Osaka, Japan for his original dishes and this dish is no different. Tuna is very popular in Japan and is the most commonly used ingredient, which is why Tatsuya has chosen it for this dish. This simple recipe is not even on Etsu's menu so can bring some originality to any dinner party.

Tatsuya began his career in Japan as a sushi chef in 1987, although previously spent three years at a fishmongers learning how to use all the knives and fillet many different species of fish. He went on to franchise his own restaurant and came third in a national competition of over 100 sushi chefs, judged on speed, quality of cut and presentation.

"I have dedicated my life to mastering various types of Japanese cooking and am still as passionate about it today as when I first started. I am now delighted to have the opportunity to prepare authentic Japanese food for the people of Liverpool," says Tatsuya.

Serves 4 as a starter
280g fresh tuna
300ml soy sauce
30g grated fresh ginger
40g grated fresh garlic
200g potato starch
30g mayonnaise
1 bunch spring onion
1 piece fresh garlic

Mix the soy sauce, grated ginger and grated garlic together to make the marinade. Cut the fresh tuna into pieces approximately 4cm x 5cm x 1cm. Heat the deep fat fryer to 170°C. Dip the tuna slices into the marinade and leave in the sauce for around 10 seconds. Then remove the tuna from the sauce and coat it in potato starch. Gently slide the tuna into the pre-heated oil and cook for four minutes ensuring golden brown. Then remove the tuna from the fryer and drain on kitchen towel.

Peel and slice the garlic thinly into small pieces and deep fry for one minute. Finally plate the tuna, dressing with mayonnaise, garlic cloves and salad.

FIVE-STAR CUISINE

FOUNDED by Mustafa and Salina Rahman in 1986, The Gulshan is Liverpool's most famous Indian restaurant.

The plaudits have been heaped upon this Aigburth Road curry house – topped by its inclusion in the Michelin Guide. The British Curry Awards, which celebrate the £3.5bn spice restaurant industry, awarded The Gulshan in Aigburth a gold 5-star plaque – for the second time. The restaurant has also been listed as one of the Top 100 Indian restaurants in the country. Amir Khan, Cliff Richard, Nicola Roberts from Girls Aloud, Monty Panesar and Hollyoaks actors have all referred to it as one of their favourite curry houses.

Recently, it has undergone something of a transformation with the downstairs restaurant decor getting a stylish makeover, and there's been a tapas and cocktail bar added upstairs too. But more importantly, the food here is impressive.

Simple, healthy, award winning

PAN-FRIED TANDOORI SEA BASS

Shajad Rahman, who helps run the award-winning Gulshan, shares one of his mother's favourite recipes with us. He says: "Having been brought up with spice as part of my daily life, the flavour of traditional Indian food is something that I feel can't be replaced by any other cuisine! "Here is a simple, healthy dish based on one of my mother's favourite recipes – pan-fried Tandoori sea bass."

Serves 2
2 sea bass fillets, 1 lemon leaf, bunch of asparagus, French beans, cherry tomatoes

For the marinade
1tsp fresh ginger paste, 1 tsp fresh garlic paste (2 cloves), 1 tsp fresh coriander paste, half a fresh lime, half a teaspoon of dry cumin powder, pinch of salt and black pepper, 1 tbsp olive oil, 1 green chilli mashed (jalapeno for more flavour less heat), half a teaspoon of fresh mustard seed paste

Use a pestle and mortar to make a paste with the ginger, garlic, coriander, lime juice, cumin, salt and black pepper, mustard seeds, oil and green chilli. Keep one teaspoon of marinade to one side for the vegetables. Place the sea bass in the marinade for an hour.

Stir-fry the asparagus, cherry tomatoes, French beans and lemon leaf in olive oil and the teaspoon of marinade, which was kept to one side. Heat some olive oil in another pan and pan-fry the sea bass. Plate with the fried vegetables and serve.

Secrets of the spices

CHICKEN TIKKA MASALA

Known as the number one love food, curry contains a vast range of aphrodisiacs including cardamom, ginger and garlic.

Mustafa Rahman of The Gulshan says: "One of the core ingredients in many Indian dishes is fenugreek, a plant that for hundreds of years was used as an aphrodisiac and a cure for impotence.

"Asian mythology often refers to the 'carnal spices' which are present in curries! Not only is chicken tikka likely to be your date's favourite food, it's also full of aphrodisiacs," Mustafa grins.

Chicken tikka masala was produced during the British Empire's control of India when one of the world's greatest cuisines found itself confronted by a palate unused to spicy food.

Legend has it that a Bangladeshi chef made it up when a British customer demanded gravy with his chicken tikka!

Serves 2

Tandoori-style chicken pieces
2 onions, finely chopped
1 large tomato, finely chopped
5 cardamom pods
2 tsp garlic, crushed to a pulp
2 tsp finely grated fresh root ginger
5 tbsp olive or groundnut oil
5cm piece of cinnamon stick
1 tsp ground cumin
1 tsp ground coriander
Quarter teaspoon of ground turmeric
1 tsp cayenne pepper
1 tbsp bright-red paprika
1 tsp tomato purée
1 tsp garam masala
150ml water
Salt

Put the oil into a large, wide pan and set it over a medium-high heat. When it is very hot, put in the cardamom pods and cinnamon stick. Stir once, then add the onions. Stir until they begin to turn brown at the edges. Add the ginger and garlic and cook, stirring for 1 minute. Add cumin, coriander, turmeric, cayenne and paprika and stir for 30 seconds.

Add the tomato, tomato purée and garam masala and cook, stirring for a minute. Pour in the water and bring to a simmer. Cover, turn the heat to low and simmer gently for 10 minutes. Taste for salt, adding about half a teaspoon or as needed.

Add the cooked chicken pieces. Raise the heat to high and fold the chicken into the sauce. The sauce should thicken and cling to the chicken pieces.

Sauce of inspiration

JOLSHANU GOSHT

Any local curry aficionado worth his poppadums will have been to The Gulshan at some stage. Expect to see many curry favourites on the menu but also a host of excellent chef specials and a good range of vegetarian options.

Here, The Gulshan shares a recipe for Jolshanu gosht, succulent lamb shank cooked in a Bengal-style, thick Jolshanu sauce.

Serves 4-6

4 lamb shanks, 6 fresh green chillies, Generous helping of fresh coriander, 2 large cinnamon sticks, Sprinkle of black pepper, 5 cardamon pods, 1 tbsp of turmeric, 1 tbsp of garam massalla, 1tsp of chilli powder or to taste, 1 tbsp ground cumin, 1 star anise, 5 cloves, 4 bay leaves, 4 tbsp chopped fresh ginger, 8 cloves crushed garlic, 6 chopped ripe tomatoes, 4 chopped onions, 1 tbsp salt or to taste, 5 tbsp yoghurt, 4 tbsp of mango chutney, 10 sun dried apricots, 400 ml water, 3-4 tbsp olive oil

Gently warm the olive oil in a large deep pan, add the onions with the garlic, ginger, salt and dry spices of cloves, star anise, cinnamon, cardamon and bay leaf.

Sauté on a low heat, softening onions to a golden brown. Add the rest of the spices after the onions have turned brown, cumin, turmeric, garam massalla and chillies. Stir gently for 5 minutes, then add 2 cups of water, the chopped tomatoes and stir another 5 minutes.

Add 400ml of water, place lamb shanks in the pan and leave on a medium to slow heat for an hour and half stirring gently. Add the yoghurt, mango chutney and apricots and simmer for a minimum hour and half until the sauce thickens and shanks have become tender. When done, plate and sprinkle with fresh coriander.

LUNYA: LARGEST IN THE UK

UNDER the creative direction of owner and executive chef, Peter Kinsella, Lunya has quickly established itself as a Mecca for Spanish food lovers. A vibrant and contemporary restaurant, Lunya is home to the largest Spanish deli in the UK and expertly blends authentic recipes, ideas and artisan ingredients from Catalunya with the finest local produce from the north west of England. Peter's passion for Spanish cuisine started in the mid 1990s when he first visited Barcelona and the chef says he is inspired by Quique Dacosta, from the Michelin-starred El Poblet restaurant, near Valencia. He explained: "Quique has been a big influence on my thinking for our menu.

"He doesn't stick to convention, which is an attitude I share when I am creating new dishes at Lunya."

A 'full Spanish'

CATALAN MIGAS

The definitive cooked Spanish breakfast. Peter Kinsella of Lunya says: "This is my own take on the classic peasant's cooked breakfast. It usually comes with sardines but I have left these out so the ingredients are similar to an English breakfast, albeit the Spanish versions, but the presentation is completely different. And just like a full English, it can be enjoyed at any time of day."

Serves 4

1 cooking chorizo
1 morcilla (Spanish black pudding)
100g of Spanish panceta
Quarter of a Spanish onion, finely chopped
Half a clove of garlic, very finely chopped
75 ml of extra virgin Arbequina olive oil
8 slices of stale bread made into
breadcrumbs
Salt and pepper
4 eggs

Chop the chorizo, morcilla and panceta into small 1 cm dice. Fry them gently in 25ml of olive oil until the juices are released.
Add the onion and garlic, finely chopped, and fry for another five minutes over a medium heat.

Moisten the breadcrumbs with a little water and add to the remaining olive oil (ensuring that the breadcrumbs are stirred well into the mixture) whilst frying for another five minutes until they are crispy. Season with salt and pepper to taste.
Serve in bowls with a poached egg on top.

Catalan salad day
ESQUEIXADA

Peter says: "This is a traditional Catalan salad that is centuries old. It is perfect for a summer lunch and uses classic Mediterranean ingredients, such as red onions, peppers and olives. These should all be available in most supermarkets, but fishmongers will have salt cod if your local supermarket doesn't."

Soak the salt cod in cold water for 12 hours, replacing the water three times. Each time, wring out the fish and rinse under a running tap, then wring it out again, before putting it in fresh water. Keep the cod and water in the fridge.

Serves 4
280g salt cod, flaked
100g red onions
100g green peppers
100g red peppers
100g black Spanish olives (Empeltre)
2 or 3 garlic cloves
20ml Núñez de Prado extra virgin olive oil
1 dessert spoon of aged sherry vinegar
40g small cherry tomatoes
20g flat leaf parsley, very finely chopped
A squeeze of fresh lemon juice

Finely chop the onions, peppers and garlic. Cut the cherry tomatoes and black olives into quarters. Tear up the salt cod into a bowl, add all of the chopped ingredients including the parsley and mix.
Add the olive oil, sherry vinegar and lemon juice. Mix together, let it marinade for an hour, and then serve.

Tip
To look at its best, serve either in a small pasta bowl with a drizzle of olive oil, or put on a small white plate in a chef's ring.

Tradition at La Vina

MONTADO DE JAMON Y GAMBAS

Growing up in a traditional Spanish family, Roberto Diaz, head chef at the vibrant tapas restaurant La Vina, believes it was impossible not to be passionate about his native cuisine.

Roberto was born and raised in the Basque city of Bilbao, Northern Spain, and from a young age was enticed by the rich flavours and variety of Spanish food in his mother's kitchen.

Serves 4

60g of Serrano ham, 250g of raw peeled king prawns (medium size), half an onion 125ml of white wine, 1 clove of garlic, 125ml of double cream, 4 slices of bread (bloomer if possible), 1tsp of parsley, salt, black pepper, 1 tbsp of olive oil

Finely chop the onion, the garlic and the parsley. In a hot pan, add the oil and onion and cook for three minutes making sure it doesn't burn. Add the Serrano ham cut into 1 by half inch slices, and cook for a further three minutes, then add the garlic, prawns and parsley and cook until the prawns turn orange.

Pour in the wine and reduce to half, then add in the double cream at a medium heat and cook until it thickens up. Season with salt and black pepper to your liking and serve on the toasted bread.

Authentic tapas

SUPREMA DE POLLO CON SALSA DE FRESAS

Today, Roberto Diaz remains heavily influenced by his Spanish roots and is passionate about working with his fellow staff at La Vina – many of whom are also Spanish – to create a delicious and authentic tapas menu.

On this dish, Roberto says: "To make the ham crispy, just remove the chicken from the foil five minutes early and place it in the oven until the ham crisps over. Make sure you don't over reduce the syrup as it will go rock solid when cold."

Serves 4

1 corn fed chicken supreme
2 slices of Serrano ham
4 strawberries
125ml of red wine
80g of sugar
120g of new potatoes
Salt
Black pepper
25ml of white wine
1 clove of garlic

Wrap the Serrano ham around the chicken supreme, place it in a piece of tin foil and create a 'bag'. Season with the salt and pepper, add the garlic and the white wine, close the foil 'bag' and place in a pre-heated oven at 180°C and cook for 20 minutes. Boil the new potatoes until soft.

Pour the red wine into a pan and bring to the boil, then add the sugar and reduce until it become syrup. Add three strawberries cut in quarters and cook for two minutes.

Once the chicken is cooked, remove it from the foil, slice the potatoes and place the supreme on top. Drizzle with the red wine and strawberry syrup and decorate with the left over strawberry.

TAPAS TAPAS...
A WAY OF LIFE

BORN out of a deep love for
Spanish life and culture, Tapas
Tapas is a family-run business
dedicated to recreating an
authentic taste of Spain at its two
restaurants in Liverpool and
Waterloo.

Head chef, Diego Hernansaez
learnt much of his trade at the
famous La Pesquera restaurant in
the glitzy town of Marbella, but it
was growing up in La Coruna,
Northern Spain where Diego's
grandmother provided his main
source of culinary inspiration.
Today many of her authentic
recipes can be found on the
specials board at Tapas Tapas.

A dish best served...
MERLUZA A LA KOSKERRA

Here Diego Hernansaez shares a recipe for Basque-style hake. This dish should be cooked in a Spanish-style Cazuela – an earthenware dish. Every Spanish kitchen has an abundance of them in all sizes - perfect for serving tapas.

Serves 4
800g of hake (in 4 slices)
300g of clams
Four cloves of garlic
150g of peas
A glass of Rioja white wine
A sprig of parsley (chopped)
2 tbsp of flour
Salt
Four asparagus spears
Olive oil
4 hard boiled eggs

Crush the garlic cloves with the flat side of a large knife so that they split in the middle (to release the maximum amount of flavour) and slowly simmer on a medium heat in a good quality Andalusian olive oil.

Dust the hake in flour (mixed with a pinch of salt) and place in the pan, allowing both sides to fry until golden brown in colour. Pour the Rioja white wine and chopped parsley, add the clams and peas and a glass of water. This should take around 15 minutes in total.

When it is done, cook the asparagus separately and use it to decorate the dish together with slices of egg.

Gentleman's Rice

ARROZ DEL SENYORET

Diego Hernansaez of Tapas Tapas says: "This Catalan-style dish is designed to be free of fish shells or 'fiddly bits' that are normally found in paella, which is where the 'gentleman's' reference comes from, as Spanish gentlemen never want to get their fingers messy!"

Serves 6

600g of Bomba paella rice
6 crayfish
6 prawns
300g of monkfish cut into cubes
200g of baby squid rings
12 mussels
2 tbsp olive oil
1 medium onion (sliced)
150g of grated tomato
1 tbsp of chopped garlic
Salt and white pepper
4 strands of saffron
2 sprigs of flat leaf parsley
1 glass of white wine
1 tsp of chopped parsley
1 tsp of paprika

Peel the seafood, keeping all the shells and offcuts of fish in order to make a fish stock later. Simmer the olive oil in a paella dish, add a pinch of salt and white pepper to sauté the prawns and crayfish. After a few minutes add the monkfish cubes and baby squid rings to the mixture. Add the garlic, paprika (be careful not to burn) and the grated tomato. Place the mussels to a separate pan and, when the shells open, remove them from the dish. Now add the rice and cook it in the pan, as if it were a stir-fry.

To make the fish stock, sauté the fish trimmings in olive oil with the sliced onion, add 1.5 litres of water, a glass of white wine and two sprigs of flat leaf parsley before simmering for 20 minutes.
Add the fish stock and de-shelled mussels to the rice. Cook over a high heat for about eight minutes before adding the saffron.
After another eight minutes, halve the heat. When the stock is almost reduced completely, turn off the heat and allow the rice to rest for five minutes (covering with a damp cloth if necessary) and then serve.

FROM AVIGNON TO CROXTETH

"WHEN I first came 'ere I was 'orrified to be confronted by Camp Coffee and brown sauce," remembers Raymond Lempereur, his accent as rich as a trembling trifle.

"I told the girl to bring the bin with the lid off."

A man of Raymond's talents was to be prized. And that was how the French chef, a member of the resistance and survivor of the German occupation, became master of culinary affairs in one of the stately homes of an England gripped by post-war austerity.

Raymond, from Avignon, arrived at Croxteth Hall in 1949 to work as chef to Lord Hugh Sefton and his wife, Lady Josephine Sefton. The following year, he was joined by his wife Elda, and together they prepared meals for one of the world's most

glamorous guest lists. The Queen Mother, with the Princesses Elizabeth and Margaret, stepped across the rolling lawns of a family seat dating back to the 13th century, as did just about every aristocrat in the land.

There was a tradition of French cooks at Croxteth Hall. Raymond says he belongs to the old school: "I learned from Escoffier, the old French master chef whose cookbook became a bible in French cuisine. Claridges and The Savoy in London are still influenced by him. To me, he is the King."

Lord Sefton had an appetite to match his 6ft 5ins presence – a breakfast of eggs, bacon, cold meats and rolls and scones would be followed by a three-dish lunch, sandwiches and cakes at 5pm, and then a five-course dinner, often with fish, meat and game. The first dinner he prepared for "his Lord-

ship" was lobster in aspic. Lady Sefton came down to see him. "It has been a long, long time since we tasted anything so fine," she told Raymond.

In 1952, Raymond saved the day – and the hall – after seeing flames coming from the Queen Anne wing. "I raised the alarm, but I must point out that I wasn't responsible for the fire!" he jokes.

"The job was very hard work, with very long hours, but it was so enjoyable. Lord Sefton was a gentleman and treated all his eight staff very well."

Lord Sefton was the seventh and last in the family line and, after his death, in 1972, Raymond and Elda ran their own delicatessen, Le Petit Gourmet in Aintree, before retiring in 1986.

In 2004, Raymond published his memoirs, Avignon to Croxteth – The Journey of Raymond Lempereur.

Ziba: Diomede scores

SCALLOPS WITH BEETROOT & ORANGE RISOTTO

For Willy Diomede, chef at Ziba at the Racquet Club, it was a desire to travel that launched his culinary career path. Originally from Bourges, Willy found himself fascinated by cooking from an early age. "My mother and father were originally from Guadeloupe. With three children, there was always something happening in the kitchen and I would help them out, peeling potatoes, going to market, or watching my mother making cakes."

After three years at catering college in Nantes, and jobs as a commis chef and chef de partie in France, it was his brother's football career, which first brought Willy to Liverpool. Bernard Diomede may have only had a brief spell with Liverpool FC, but Willy was captivated by the language, culture – and his wife, Dee, who he met here.

"Travelling around the world has opened my mind and I love trying new things out, learning and adapting. This recipe reflects the French appreciation of food – you don't need extravagance, just simple produce, a knowledge of what colours and flavours work together, and a bit of imagination."

Serves 4 as a starter

12 scallops
150g Arborio rice
1 medium or 2 small shallots
1 clove garlic
Half a glass of white wine
1 pint stock (chicken or vegetable)
4 small cooked beetroots
Juice and zest of half an orange
Light olive oil
Butter
Salt & pepper
Dill, finely chopped

Cut the beetroot into small pieces and place in a blender with the orange zest, orange juice and a little water. Blend until it forms a smooth liquid. Leave to one side.

Cut the shallots and garlic finely. Heat the olive oil in a pan and cook the shallot and garlic gently for about 3 to 4 minutes. Add the rice and stir for 2 or 3 minutes so that the rice starts to look slightly translucent. Add the wine and keep stirring. Once the wine has reduced, add a ladle of stock and a pinch of salt and pepper to taste. Continue stirring all the time and keep the heat low. Allow the stock to be absorbed each time before adding another ladleful of stock. Keep stirring and adding stock for approximately 15 minutes or until the rice is cooked but with a slight bite. Remove from the heat and add a knob of butter. Place a lid on the pan and allow to rest for 2 to 3 minutes. Add the beetroot puree to the risotto just before serving.

Season the scallops both sides. Heat a frying pan and add a little olive oil. Sear the scallops on a high heat for approximately 2 minutes each side. Serve the scallops with the risotto and sprinkle with the finely chopped dill.

Something to share

TARTE TATIN

"In France, food is a social event – we love to entertain and enjoy conversation while we are eating," says Willy Diomede, chef at Liverpool's Racquet Club. "The door is always open and there is always something to share, whether it's food or ideas."

"The famous story behind the Tarte Tatin, tells of the Tatin sisters, who accidentally dropped an apple tarte while rushing about in the kitchen. One Tatin sister picked it up and rearranged it as best she could – upside down – to go in the oven. When the baked tarte was turned out with its pastry on the bottom, the Tarte Tatin was born."

Serves 4
2kg apples
(Golden Delicious/Pink Lady)
160g sugar
80g butter
250g puff pastry

For the caramel
100g water
100g sugar

Heat the sugar and water gently in an oven-proof frying pan until it thickens and becomes golden brown with a syrupy texture. Remove from the heat and allow to cool by placing the base of the pan into cold water. Leave to one side.

Peel the apples and cut into wedges (approximately 8 pieces per apple). Melt the butter in a separate pan and add the sugar and the apple wedges and cook slowly until the apples start to turn golden brown.

Place the apple wedges onto the caramel in the oven-proof frying pan so that the wedges are placed close to each other forming a circular pattern and filling the pan.

Roll out the pastry and cover the pan, trimming off any excess pastry. Cook for approximately 45 minutes at 160°C/gas mark 3.

Remove from the oven and place a plate that is larger than pan over the top of the pastry, and turning the pan vertically, carefully allow any remaining caramel to pour away. Turn the pie upside down so that the pastry is now on the plate, and remove the pan carefully so as not to displace any of the apple.

Serve warm with vanilla ice cream or fresh cream.

A piece of Paris

FILET DE BEOUF AU ROQUEFORT

Something of a local institution, the bustling surroundings of Bistro Jacques, Bistro Franc and Bistro Pierre have been recreating a little piece of Paris in the heart of Liverpool for the past seven years.

And that's partly thanks to executive chef, Craig Sallery. A master of French cuisine, Craig was born and raised in Liverpool and for the past five years has been at the helm of the kitchens of these popular city eateries. Craig says: "I fell in love with the French classics while training at catering college when I was 16 and ever since have been inspired by chefs like Anthony Bourdain and my father, Peter, to create classic dishes with the fresh produce that arrives at the Bistros everyday."

Craig adds: "This dish is so simple to make yet so rich and tasty that it goes down well in all our restaurants when it makes an appearance on the monthly changing menu."

Serves 4

4 fillets of beef, about 7oz each
4 pieces of smoked streaky bacon
8 large field mushrooms
250g of Roquefort (cut into 4 pieces)
1 pint of beef stock (reduced by half)
1 pint of Merlot (reduced by half)
Salt and pepper
1 clove of garlic (peeled and sliced)
3 tbsp of butter
2 tbsp of flour
Olive oil

Wrap the beef fillets with the streaky bacon, season with salt and pepper, and refrigerate. Mix the beef stock and wine together, then simmer on a low heat, and reduce again by half.

While the sauce is reducing, roast the mushrooms with the garlic in a hot oven (220°C). When cooked, set aside and keep warm. For the fillets melt 1 tbsp of butter in a pan with a drop of olive oil until it begins to foam. Place the fillets in the pan and cook to your preference on a medium heat.

Top with the Roquefort and place under a medium grill to melt. Mix the remaining butter with the flour to form a smooth dough and whisk this mix into the simmering sauce. If it becomes too thick simply add some more wine and then simmer for about five minutes to cook out the flour.

Assemble all the prepared ingredients as follows: Put the mushrooms on the plate; pour the sauce over the mushrooms and top it all off with the delicious cheesy fillet steak.

Bistro classic
COQ AU VIN

Craig Sallery, executive chef of Bistros Jacques, Franc and Pierre, says: "This classic braise of chicken has many variations according to the region of France that it is made in. For example Coq au Riesling is made using local wine from the Alsace region but for the purpose of this recipe we will use the more widely used Burgundy."

Serves 4

1 tbsp of olive oil
1 large free range chicken, cut into 8
1 large onion (peeled and chopped)
3 cloves of garlic (peeled and sliced)
1 large carrot (peeled and chopped)
125g of smoked streaky bacon (cut into small pieces)
20 button mushrooms
Salt and pepper
1 sprig of thyme
1 sprig of parsley
3 bay leaves
1 bottle of Burgundy wine
A double brandy
1 tbsp of flour
2 tbsp of butter
100ml good quality chicken stock
20 new potatoes

Using an oven proof casserole dish, heat a tablespoon of olive oil and a tablespoon of butter. Melt the butter over a medium heat and let it foam, add the carrot and onion and cook for a few minutes until it starts to colour. Next add the bacon and when it begins to brown, add the garlic – if it is sliced thinly enough it should just melt, try not to colour it – and cook it for a further three to four minutes.

Remove the vegetables and bacon from the dish but leave the fat in. Turn up the heat on the pan then add four pieces of the chicken and let it brown for about four minutes. When they are golden turn them over and cook for a further four minutes and remove from the pan and repeat with the last four pieces.

Return everything to the pan, add the brandy and flambé – be careful now! Once the alcohol has burnt off, season the pot with the salt, pepper and herbs and add the wine (reserving a glass to prepare the mushrooms) and chicken stock slowly.
Cover the casserole dish and place in a medium oven (180°C) for about an hour and a half. While the chicken is cooking, prepare the mixture to thicken the sauce. To do this, mix one tablespoon of flour and one of butter together until combined thoroughly and place in the fridge till required later.
In a separate saucepan, cook the mushrooms by adding one tablespoon of butter, the remaining glass of wine and season. Simmer for 20 minutes.

Boil the new potatoes for approximately 15 minutes until soft. When the chicken is cooked, remove from the pot and keep warm. Strain the sauce into a clean pan and add any remaining liquid from the mushrooms. Bring to the boil, then reduce, add the thickening mixture and simmer for five minutes. Add the chicken and mushroom to reheat. Serve with more of that delicious burgundy and melt some butter over the potatoes.

DECADES OF TRADITION

CHRISTAKIS Georgiou may only have been in Liverpool for 13 years, but he is the heir to a city dining tradition going back decades.

And as both owner and head chef of his Greek taverna in York Street, he is in a position to keep up standards that have made his place, originally named Renos, a favourite for Liverpool diners since the 1970s.

It's been a family business in the proper sense of the world. Renos Vasilianis was a leader of the Greek Cypriot community in Liverpool who made his name first at Zorba's in Leece Street.

Then he branched out on his own, setting up Renos in York Street, a little Greek island in the district now known as Ropewalks. Renos sold the business and retired to Cyprus, but son-in-law Christakis bought it back in the 1990s to re-establish the family link. He arrived in Liverpool as a manager at Caesar's Palace, and took over Renos after a spell at Aki's in Lark Lane.

"We were very happy it came back in the family," he recalls.

Family favourite
MOUSSAKA

Christakis' recipes include what for many people is their first taste of Greek cooking – moussaka. As with all Greek and Middle Eastern cookery, if you have a favourite spice or herb which you think will blend in with the rest, feel free to experiment. There are, after all, as many versions of moussaka as there are Greek kitchens.

Just build on the basics of aubergines, tomatoes, minced lamb, cinnamon and a slightly nutmeg-flavoured bechamel sauce.
For the cheese, you can use Greek kefalotiro, or substitute pecorino romano, parmesan or cheddar.

Serves 4
1 large onion, finely chopped
650g lamb mince
2 large potatoes, peeled and sliced lengthways
Quarter teaspoon of cinnamon
400g chopped tomatoes
2 courgettes, sliced across
4 medium-sized aubergines
Splash of white wine
Bechamel sauce
Grated cheese
Parsley, salt and pepper

Slice the aubergines into 1cm thick slices. Place in a drainer and sprinkle with salt. Leave for 30 minutes to draw out any bitter juices. Fry the potatoes, courgettes, and aubergines and then drain the oil.

Fry the mince with onions, chopped tomatoes, parsley, salt, pepper and cinnamon, with white wine, until the meat is browned and cooked.

Lay the vegetables in a tray, potatoes in the bottom, then the courgettes, and aubergines on the top. Drain any excess oil from the mince and place the meat on the top of the vegetables. Finish it with bechamel sauce on top and some grated cheese. Cook it for about 30-45 minutes in a medium oven at 180°C until the sauce becomes golden brown.

Greek salad

Stifado

Straight from the taverna

STIFADO

GREEK SALAD

This traditional Greek salad is simplicity itself, while the beef stew is a staple of every taverna across Greece and Cyprus – with each of them claiming to make the truest version there is.

Greek and Middle Eastern food still depends very much on traditions passed down. To get the full authenticity, hunt down a Greek or Middle Eastern delicatessen, but acceptable substitutes can usually be found in any well-stocked supermarket.

Remember that this is hearty country cookery and not fine dining, so don't be afraid to tweak the ingredients a little. A pinch of oregano goes well in the Greek salad, while the stifado lends itself well to a slow cooker, possibly with the addition of a dash of tomato puree or a chopped tomato for some extra flavour.

Serves 4
For the Stifado
1.5 kg silverside beef
100g plain flour
Half a bottle of good, rich red wine
2 tbsp red wine vinegar
800g baby onions or shallots
One cinnamon stick, broken in half
3 bay leaves
2 cloves
2 garlic clove
1 tsp cumin
Salt and freshly ground black pepper

Stifado

Cut the beef into cubes, and toss in the flour before frying in olive oil. When the meat gets brown, empty out the oil, add red wine to cover the meat and cook slowly. Add the onions and the cinnamon, cumin, salt and pepper, bay leaves, chopped garlic and two cloves. Add some water if it's needed and some more wine.

Cook it for at least one 1hr 30mins in a moderate oven of 160°C, Gas Mark 3, or even longer, as long as it does not dry out and you can resist the delicious smell from the oven. Serve with crusty bread or potatoes flavoured with rosemary.

Serves 4
For the Greek salad
One small lettuce
3 medium tomatoes
1 cucumber
Half a red onion
1 green pepper
150g feta cheese
50g Greek kalamata olives
Olive oil
Red wine vinegar

Greek salad

Roughly chop the lettuce and cut the tomatoes and cucumber into cubes of around 2cm. Finely slice the red onion. Deseed and cut the green pepper into strips. Cube the feta cheese. Mix all the ingredients, without the olives, and toss in a traditional olive oil and red wine vinegar dressing. Use the olives as garnish.

A taste OF ITALY

BY the late 18th century, Italian masons and other skilled craftsmen, such as gilders and carvers, had begun settling in Liverpool.

They were followed by doctors, opticians, engineers, mariners and musicians. But their numbers were quite small. Some of the highly skilled tradesmen travelled across Europe from job to job. However, Italians began arriving in greater numbers in the late 19th and early 20th centuries. Many came from the mountain villages between Rome and Naples. The streets around Scotland Road soon became known as 'Little Italy'.

In the 1950s a National Coal Board deal attracted hundreds of Italians to work in the Lancashire pit towns, including Bold and Sutton Manor, St Helens. Their country's economy had not yet begun its post-war recovery.

So, from the sunshine and swollen watermelons of southern Italy and Sicily, they found themselves with torches on their helmets, hacking out coal or running the trolleys in those depths where there has never been a dawn. Others broke the frozen ground with their shovels and pick-axes on farms. Whether they were overground or underground, it was hard work for tough men.

Giuseppe Sereni, 75, from Tuscany, didn't like the English food. "It was terrible," he says.

"There were so many cakes and sweets. We were used to spaghetti and macaroni, fruit and vegetables. Some of the Italians were so unhappy about the diet that they persuaded the local doctors to issue prescriptions for olive oil which was supplied in the chemists' shops.

"Of course, we had to learn the English language and we went to a school. It was a lovely country. We met some nice people and everyone welcomed us."

BOLD PRINCIPLES

HEAD chef Maurizio Pellegrini and his partner Rosaria Crolla, run The Italian Club and its sister Fish restaurant, both on bustling Bold Street.

Maurizio believes the success of the Clubs are partly due to their resistance to 'dumbing down' the Italian dishes they serve.

"We make authentic Italian cuisine and real Italian biscuits and desserts. We don't want to make our Italian dishes more 'British'. Customers know that when they come in here they will be transported to a café in a square in a beautiful Italian city, and will be eating exactly what the Italians eat."

Rosaria says: "At the Italian Club we welcome families and I love the noise and buzz that these customers create in our café."

Rome from home

SPAGHETTI CARBONARA

Spaghetti carbonara, a traditional dish from the Lazio region of Italy, near Rome, is a favourite on the specials board at The Italian Club.

Maurizio says: "This dish takes a certain amount of concentration to get right. It is important to use the cream to stop the eggs from scrambling while pasta such as spaghetti is also helpful for this."

Serves 2
500g spaghetti
200g smoked pancetta - diced
50g butter
100g grated parmesan
5 egg yolks
2 whole eggs
100g single cream
Salt and pepper to taste

For the sauce, heat a pan and add the butter and then the pancetta. Let it pan-fry on a low heat until brown. Don't let the butter burn – if it does add a little water. Whisk the eggs, parmesan and cream in a bowl until the mixture has combined. Boil a pan of water. Add a little salt and put the spaghetti in the pan. Cook for 7-8 minutes until the pasta is 'al dente' – if you bend the pasta you should still see a little white inside. Drain the pasta.

Add the pasta to the pancetta and a little of the water from the pasta. Mix together on a low heat adding the cream sauce. When creamy, after 2-3 minutes take off the heat. Add salt and cracked black pepper to taste. Serve with a cold glass of Pinot Grigio.

Il Forno: Passion on a plate

OSSOBUCO ALLA MILANESE

Passionate about great Italian food and wine, served in a vibrant atmosphere by people who care about true service, Il Forno searches Italy for the very best of ingredients.

Its cured meats, cheeses, pasta and olive oil are all sourced directly from local, artisan producers in Parma, Salerno and Basilicata. The head chef, Paolo Cillo, was born in the picturesque town of Potenza, Southern Italy, where he discovered his love for cooking at the tender age of 11.

"I loved being in the family kitchen and really enjoyed watching my family cook and helping to prepare dishes. When I was older, I helped in the kitchen of my family's local trattoria – which only further ignited my passion for food and cooking."

Paolo won a place to train at the prestigious Etoile Cookery school in Italy, and months after completing this training, he was recruited as head chef at Il Forno.

Serves 3

Cheesecloth and kitchen twine
3 whole veal shanks (about 1 pound per shank), trimmed
1 sprig of fresh rosemary
1 sprig of fresh thyme
1 bay leaf
2 whole cloves
Sea salt
Freshly ground black pepper
All purpose flour
Half a cup of extra virgin olive oil
1 small onion, diced into cubes
1 small carrot, diced into cubes
1 stalk celery, diced into cubes
1 tbsp tomato paste
1 cup of dry white wine
3 cups of veal or chicken stock
3 tbsp of chopped, flat leaf parsley
1 tbsp of lemon zest

Place the rosemary, thyme, bay leaf and cloves into the cheesecloth and secure with twine. This will be your bouquet garni.
Pat the veal shanks dry with paper towels to remove any excess moisture. Secure the meat to the bone with the kitchen twine. Season each shank with salt and freshly ground pepper. Dust the shanks in flour, shaking off any excess.

In a large Dutch oven pot, heat the olive oil until smoking. Add the veal shanks to the hot pan and brown all sides (about 3 minutes per side). Remove the shanks and put to one side.

In the same pot, add the onion, carrot and celery. Season with salt and sauté until soft and translucent (about 8 minutes). Add the tomato paste and mix well. Return the shanks to the pan and add the white wine. Reduce the liquid by half (about 5 minutes). Add the bouquet garni and chicken stock and bring to a boil. Reduce the heat to low, cover the pan and simmer for about one and a half hours or until the meat is falling off the bone. Check every 15 minutes, turning them gently and adding more chicken stock as necessary. The shank should be submerged by two thirds of the cooking liquid. Once cooked, carefully remove the shanks from the pot and place in a decorative serving platter. Cut off the kitchen twine and discard. Remove and discard bouquet garni. The dish is best served with saffron risotto. Place the Ossobuco on top of the risotto, pouring all the juices over the shanks. Garnish with chopped parsley and lemon zest.

Savouring the San Carlo buzz

SPAGHETTI WITH LOBSTER SAUCE

An award-winning family business renowned for its authentic Italian cuisine and speciality fish dishes, at San Carlo customer preferences are well catered for and the wine list is 90% Italian.

Open noon 'til late, the buzzing atmosphere makes it a popular hangout for celebrities and sports personalities.

Serves 4
2 x 700g live lobsters
125ml extra virgin olive oil
1 garlic clove finely chopped
1 tbsp finely chopped flat leaf parsley
plus extra for garnish
400g cherry tomatoes, halved
Salt
1 red fresh chili, seeded and finely chopped
350g spaghetti

Bring a large saucepan of salted water to the boil and plunge the lobsters, head first, into it. Return to the boil and cook the lobsters for 5 minutes. Remove the lobsters from the pot and plunge them into cold water to cool them quickly. When cold, twist off the claws, crack them and remove the meat. Cut open the shell, cutting down the length of the soft underside. Remove the meat from the shell, discarding the stomach sac and dark central vein, and cut the meat into cubes. Wash and dry the shells in the oven and reserve.

In a frying pan heat the oil then add the garlic, parsley and chili and briefly fry. Add the halved cherry tomatoes and cook for a few minutes. Add the lobster meat and stir adding a little water to the pan. Season with salt.

Meanwhile, bring a large saucepan of lightly salted water to the boil. Cook the spaghetti al dente. Drain and add to the lobster mixture, mix in well. Place a lobster shell on each plate and fill with the spaghetti and lobster sauce. Decorate with a little parsley and serve at once.

A taste of Egypt
CHICKEN BOREK

Offering a flavour of Egypt in the heart of south Liverpool, Sakara bar and restaurant offers an authentic Middle Eastern experience. Bringing a new and exciting cuisine to the city, Sakara has built up a reputation for its unique menu, chilled-out ambience and friendly atmosphere. Chef Simon Mayne and proprietor Claire O'Regan have created some fabulous dishes including delights such as Egyptian tagine, chicken borek and chilli beef and firecracker rice.

Makes 8
3 red chillies, 5 cloves of garlic, 200g of toasted pine nuts, 1½ tablespoons cumin, 3 chicken breasts, salt and pepper, filo pastry, sweet chilli dip, cucumber to garnish

Blend the chillies, garlic, pine nuts and cumin in a food processor. Dice the chicken breasts and add to the mixture. Season with salt and pepper and blend until you have a smooth mixture.

Take the filo pastry and cut into large squares. Lay one sheet down and brush with melted butter, lay another sheet on top and continue until you have three sheets layered and buttered.

Divide the chicken mixture into 8 equal portions and roll out one portion and lay across the filo pastry, leaving one inch at each side. Fold in each side and then begin to roll up the pastry, brushing with melted butter as you go.

Bake in a preheated oven, 220°C/gas mark 7, for 13-15 minutes until golden and crisp.

Halve the borek and serve with a sweet chilli dip and cucumber salad.

MERSEYSIDE SHINES WITH FIRST MICHELIN STAR

GROWING up in Huyton on a diet of fish fingers and baked beans, Marc Wilkinson never dreamed he would one day be one of the country's most celebrated chefs, earning Merseyside its first Michelin star.

Tucked away in Oxton, Fraiche has been a bit of a hidden gem, at least as far as the rest of the country was concerned. But, since the small, 20-cover restaurant was awarded a Michelin star, the owner and patron has faced an avalanche of interest.

"It's amazing the difference an accolade makes," says Marc, sounding a touch bemused. "It's been a mad house. The phones haven't stopped ringing.

"When we won three rosettes, we had a little bit of a surge, but it was nothing like winning the Michelin star. It's been a hard struggle to get recognised, especially with it being in Merseyside, trying to shake off the stigma for our dining. But it's my home, so I stuck with it."

After his first job in a hotel kitchen, Marc went on to work at the Michelin-starred Winteringham House, then Midsummer House in Cambridge and in Canada, before setting up a successful restaurant in Essex. But, when it came to opening a restaurant he calls his 'baby', he came back to Merseyside. He bought the restaurant freehold, refurbished it himself and set about inventing technically-advanced, tour de force menus of modern French style.

Marc says: "We are so individual here, some people do not get it - people who go out just for sustenance and to fill up. Fraiche is not about that, we're about new flavour combinations and doing different things."

Marc has now been named one of the country's leading chefs. Along with Southport's Marcus Wareing who is based at the Berkeley hotel in London, Marc was among 10 top cooks featured in the 2010 Good Food Guide and highlighted by food lovers.

Marc admits he is pleased to be recognised, but insisted he would continue to devote himself to developing his Oxton restaurant.

He says: "My passion is cooking and I'm always in the kitchen - that's my personal choice, it's what I trained to do all those years. The evolution of food is the exciting bit for me."

He can no more stop his mind dreaming up new or improved dishes than he can stop breathing, so keeping Fraiche fresh won't be a problem.

"We like to keep evolving," he says.

NEW GOAL FOR STEVIE G

SOUTHPORT'S Warehouse Brasserie has long been a magnet for Merseyside's football stars.

But now Liverpool FC and England captain Steven Gerrard has gone one step further and bought a share in his favourite restaurant.

Gerrard has joined forces with hotelier Paul Adams to launch the new venue, now known as the Warehouse Kitchen and Bar.

Steven, as a shareholder in the venture, said: "If you look back at any interviews I have done where they've asked me about my favourite restaurant, and I've done a lot over the years, I've always said the Warehouse.

"I've been eating there for years because I love the food and the atmosphere, so it's genuinely exciting to become its co-owner with Paul.

"I certainly don't want to just be the 'celebrity' face of the restaurant. This is not a theme bar, it's about great food, great surroundings and making it a place that people really want to come back to."

The venue has had a major refurbishment and features a new menu, designed by Paul Adams and head chef Tom Lowe, including the likes of fish goujons and chips, moules mariniere, and blackened cod as well as new additions like chilli and chocolate pork belly.

Prior to heading up the kitchen at the Warehouse, Tom has worked at restaurants across the country including Heathcotes in Preston and Manchester and The Heights Restaurant in London.

Oriental twist

BLACK COD IN MISO

Serves 4

185ml mirin
125ml sake
225g white miso paste
225g sugar
4 black cod fillets
Pickled ginger slices

Tom Lowe, head chef at Warehouse Kitchen and Bar, shares his recipe for black cod in miso. The fish will need to marinate in the fridge for two to three days – so plan ahead!

In a medium saucepan, combine the mirin and sake. Boil for 20 seconds over a medium heat to evaporate the alcohol.

Add the miso paste and stir with a wooden spoon until it dissolves Add the sugar, raise the heat to high, and stir continuously until it has dissolved completely. Remove the pan from the heat and leave at room temperature until the mixture has cooled completely. Put the cod fillets in a dish or a bowl and slather them with the miso, saving a few spoonfuls of the sauce in a small covered bowl in the refrigerator to serve. Cover tightly with cling film and refrigerate for two to three days.

When you are ready to cook, preheat the oven to 200°C/gas 6 and pre heat the grill. Lightly wipe off any excess miso clinging to the fillets, but don't rinse it off. Place the fish under the grill and cook until the surface browns, then transfer to a baking dish and cook in the oven until the fish is opaque in its centre, about 10-15 minutes more.

Reheat the reserved sauce in a small saucepan, and serve the fillets hot with radish and pickled ginger.

Chocolate indulgence

BLACK FOREST SUNDAE

For a truly indulgent dessert, try this recipe for Black Forest sundae with chocolate sauce, from Tom Lowe, head chef at Warehouse Kitchen and Bar.

Serves 6
120g melted butter
50g cocoa powder
2 whole eggs
60g plain flour
50g chopped nuts
50g chopped white chocolate
120g milk chocolate melted
Whipped cream with added vanilla pod and icing sugar
1 jar Griottine cherries
Cherry ice cream
3 Flakes

For the chocolate sauce
125ml double cream
100g milk chocolate

Preheat the oven to 180°C. Line your baking tray with greaseproof paper. Beat the sugar and eggs together until pale. Melt the butter and fold into the egg mix.

Mix together the flour and cocoa powder and sieve into the egg mixture. Continue to whisk. Add the melted chocolate and continue to whisk.

Once mixed together, add the nuts and white chocolate. Pour into your lined baking tray and bake for 30-40 minutes at 180°C. Boil the cream and add chocolate, mix until melted.

Building your Sundae
In your sundae glasses, place the cherries in the bottom, then layer pieces of chocolate brownie, chocolate sauce and whipped cream, a scoop of cherry ice cream, and start layers again, finishing with the whipped cream.

Top with a cherry and half a flake.

A Hard Day's bite

CHICKEN SUPREME WITH LOBSTER MOUSSE

Most of the Beatles connections at the Hard Day's Night Hotel in Liverpool are pretty obvious, but the title of the restaurant may have some diners scratching their heads. Blakes is actually named after the artist Peter Blake, whose album sleeve for Sgt Pepper's Lonely Hearts Club Band is one of the defining images of The Beatles' later period.

Executive head chef Andrew Scott has gone for a seasonal menu with a homely feel to it: "The kind of food I'd like to go out and eat myself," he explains. Here, Andrew shares his recipe for chicken supreme with lobster mousse, crab and potato salad, buttered baby vegetables, and chive beurre blanc. He says: "This dish is inspired by the good old surf'n'turf that I used to enjoy during my travels around the UK. Here I have decided to put my own little twist on the irresistible poultry and shellfish combination. In this recipe I have used lobster, but prawns and crayfish are a cheaper but no less delicious option. Most supermarkets now sell tinned crab meat and lobster meat, but it depends on your budget."

Serves 4

4 chicken supremes (200g skin on bone in)
50g lobster
50g fresh salmon
1 egg yolk
50g crab meat
200g new potatoes
1 small red onion
2 shallots
125ml white wine
125ml double cream
100g butter, divided into 4
50g chives
Salt and pepper
Sunflower oil
100g mange tout or green beans
100g baby corn
100g baby carrots

For the mousse, you will need the lobster, salmon and egg yolk. Put the lobster and salmon into a food processor and blend for 1 minute. Season by adding a good pinch of salt and pepper, and add the egg yolk before blending again for 10 to 15 seconds.

With the chicken skin side facing down, take a sharp knife and make an incision along the side of the chicken from top to bottom to make a pocket. Be careful not to break the flesh or skin. Divide the mousse evenly and, using a spoon, fill the pocket of the chicken. Brush the chicken skin with oil, season with salt and pepper and roast for 20 to 25 minutes until golden brown.
For the sauce, add a little oil in a pan and cook the shallots until transparent, then add the white wine and reduce the volume by half. Next, add the cream and reduce by half again. Season and put to one side. For the potato salad, pre-cook the vegetables and the new potatoes separately and leave to cool. Finely chop the red onion and the chives, and roughly dice the new potato and leave to one side. Put 25g of butter into a pan followed by the red onion and new potatoes. Add the crab meat and season. Finally, add the chives and gently heat until the potato salad is warm. You're now ready to bring all the separate elements together and plate up!

Bring the sauce back to the boil then remove from the heat. Add 50g of butter and stir until completely melted. It is important that you do not reheat the sauce as it will split. Add the finely chopped chives to finish. In a pan of boiling water reheat the vegetables for 1 minute and drain. In a bowl put the last 25g of butter and vegetables, and toss until coated.

Cut diagonally along the length of the chicken and place on top of the potato salad and vegetables. Pour a little of the sauce on and round the chicken. Garnish with some more chives.

A crackling starter

MAPLE SYRUP BRAISED PORK BELLY

Andrew Scott, executive head chef at Blakes, within Liverpool's Hard Day's Night Hotel, says: "I love fusion cooking and so created this dish based upon sweet and sour pork, a dish that I love. I took the classic Chinese dish and put an English twist on it, to make either a cracking starter or a light main."

Serves 8 starters or 4 mains
1kg pork belly with skin (but ask the butcher to remove skin)
250g clear honey
250g maple syrup
100g dark brown sugar
4 green apples
12 walnut halves
100g salt

Pre-heat oven to 150°C. Heavily salt the pork belly skin, place between 2 sheets of greaseproof paper then place on a baking tray and add another tray on top – this will keep your crackling to an even thickness. Cook in oven for 1 hour.

After an hour remove the top tray and top sheet of greaseproof paper and cook for a further hour. The skin should then be brittle enough to snap. Depending on the oven this might need a little longer. Allow to cool and then break into equal pieces, either 4 or 8 depending on whether you're using the dish as a starter or a main.

In a pan on the stove put the honey, maple syrup and the sugar and heat until boiling. Leave this to simmer for 5 minutes. The sugar should have completely dissolved. Pour just enough of the syrup over the walnuts to cover and allow to cool. Score the pork belly lightly like a chess board and place on greaseproof paper in a deep roasting tray. Pour the remaining syrup over the meat and, again, cover with another piece of greaseproof paper. Place another tray on top (this will stop the meat drying up) and cook for 2 to 3 hours, basting the meat every 30 minutes.

Once cooked, put something heavy on the top tray to press the flavour into the meat and help keep it even, and allow to cool. Remove from the tray, making sure to keep the syrup, and portion into equal sizes (4 or 8). With the syrup, remove the visible layer of fat and put to one side.

Peel, core and roughly dice the apples, place in a pan with a little water (do not add sugar, you want the apples to be sour) and cook until the apples start to fall apart. Blend until smooth in a food processor and allow to cool.

To serve, reheat the pork belly in a medium hot oven (180°C) for about 8-10 minutes. Spoon 2 to 3 tablespoons of apple puree onto the centre of the plate. Make a small incision into the pork belly. Put the reheated pork belly on top of the apple puree. Place the crackling into the incision. Garnish with sticky walnuts and the remaining syrup.

Living it up
LAMB SHOULDERS

Chic, upbeat and welcoming, The Living Room is a unique restaurant and bar, which made Liverpool its home 10 years ago. The Living Room offers a wide range of high quality food and drink choices, brought to the table with an award-winning level of service. An extensive à la carte menu is supplemented by daily specials and monthly chef's plates from head chef John O'Brien, who creates regionally inspired dishes from local produce, or with local significance.

Serves 5
5 lamb shoulders
1 onion
Half a leek
1 carrot
Half a stick of celery
7 cloves of garlic
3 bay leaves
500ml demi-glace sauce (or gravy)
1 sprig of rosemary
125ml red wine
2 pinches of salt and pepper
Olive oil
1 litre water
Vegetable stock

Chop the onion, leek, carrot, celery, and garlic, into large pieces. Heat a frying pan and add the olive oil. Season the lamb joints and add to the pan, once sealed place the lamb into a colander to drain off any excess fat. In the same pan, caramelise the vegetables, add red wine and bring to the boil.

Add water, vegetable stock and bring back to the boil. Place the lamb in a metal tray, pour over the vegetable and sauce stock, cover with foil and cook for approx 60-90 minutes at 180°C.

Light and spicy
THAI SALMON FISHCAKES

Serves 5

350g salmon trimmings
1 egg white
3 pea sized blobs of Wasabi
3 spring onion slivers 1 pinch of finely
chopped coriander
250g breadcrumbs
125g mashed potato
1.5 dessertspoon of Tom Yum Paste
1 pinch of salt and pepper
3 cloves of garlic, finely chopped
1 tsp of dried chilli flakes
100g grated ginger

Cut the salmon into 1cm cubes, place half in a mixing bowl and add egg white. Pulse or blend for 30 seconds (just enough to break the salmon up).

Place over the other half of the salmon and the rest of the ingredients and gently bring together. Leave to rest for 10 minutes. Separate into equal measures, roll into balls then flatten into cakes. Store for 20 minutes in the fridge to set.

Heat some groundnut oil in a frying pan over a moderate heat and fry the cakes until golden brown. Serve with a sweet chilli sauce dip and lime wedges for squeezing.

Secret of the Incas at Peninsula

BUTTERNUT SQUASH RISOTTO

South America is a world away from New Brighton, but it was a secret of the Incas that gave one Wirral chef a veggie recipe for success. Ross Gray from the Peninsula Dining Rooms impressed judges at the Vegetarian Chef of the Year 2010 competition with his quinoa risotto. A hardy plant which flourishes at high altitudes and in areas of low rainfall, quinoa was for centuries a staple food of the Incas. The South Americans eat it like porridge but it can be used as the main ingredient in a wide variety of vegetarian and vegan meals and as a meat alternative.

Ross's unusual dish was named joint winner in the Vegetarian Chef of the Year competition, an event organised by Sarah Kearns and Mo Hall, the team behind Bebington-based cookery school Vegi-Table. Ross says: "I'd heard loads about quinoa, but I'd never used it in the restaurant, so I bought a packet from Asda and gave it a go. I was really impressed.

"We always try to make our vegetarian options as interesting and imaginative as possible. I find that a lot of vegetarians are excellent chefs in their own right. They're used to finding new ingredients and trying different flavours and textures, so it keeps me on top of my game. I like a challenge."

Serves 4

1 packet quinoa
1 butternut squash
1 large white leek
1 handful pumpkin seeds
Vegetable stock
Red amaranth (for garnish)
Unsalted butter
Veggie parmesan or goats cheese

Wash the quinoa until the water runs clear. Cook in lightly seasoned water for approx 10-12 minutes until it's tender but still has a slight bite. Spread out on a tray to cool quickly. Next, peel and dice the butternut squash. Dice the whites of the leek and keep to the side.

Make up some vegetable stock. Gently roast the butternut squash until it is tender. Toast off pumpkin seeds in the oven until golden and nutty. If you are using cheese, grate or dice it down and return to the fridge.

Place a pan on a medium heat and lightly oil. Cook off your leek whites until they are translucent, then slowly put the quinoa in and mix well. Gradually add vegetable stock.

When it is gently coming to the boil, add your cooked butternut squash and then put in some diced butter, which gives a lovely creamy taste. If you are using the cheese, omit the butter. When it looks nearly ready, add in the toasted seeds and serve. Garnish with the amaranth, which has a lovely sweet taste.

Homely Hilton

GOOSNARCH CHICKEN BREAST & LEG WITH CREAMED CABBAGE, SHALLOT AND MUSHROOMS

High-ups in the Hilton empire may raise an eyebrow or two at the inclusion of Scouse, Liverpool Tarts and Wet Nellies on the Liverpool menu, but executive chef Matt Burns says they sit comfortably alongside the likes of his Goosnargh chicken breast and leg dish.

"It's all about local heritage," he explains. "Liverpool's a really proud city, they're proud of their products and their heritage. For us not to feature some traditional Liverpool dishes would be blasphemy, really."

The Hilton menu has a distinct local flavour and it goes almost without saying that food is as fresh as humanly possible, with the aim being to source at least 75% of the ingredients from within 50 miles of the hotel. That means, for example, lamb from Hesketh Bank near Southport, poultry from Goosnargh in Lancashire and fish from Fleetwood. "We're trying to bring fresh, traditional, approachable food at a price that people aren't going to be scared of in a comfortable environment," says Matt.

Serves 2
1 whole chicken
Thyme
1 lemon (juiced)
Salt and pepper
50g chopped pancetta
10g butter
1 chilli seeded and chopped
Duck fat
50g flour
1 egg
Panko bread crumbs

For the creamed cabbage
1 Savoy cabbage, sliced
1 tbsp Dijon mustard
50ml chicken stock
100ml cream
15g butter
Salt and pepper

For the shallot and mushroom
200g mixed mushrooms
1 onion, diced
1 tsp tarragon chopped
Reduced chicken stock
Crème fraiche
1 or 2 whole roasted shallots per person

Break the chicken in to breast and legs. Remove the thigh for use in a separate dish. With the breast – season with salt and pepper, mix thyme with butter and chopped pancetta. Rub the breasts with butter and tie in cling film into a sausage shape. Boil or steam for 45 minutes.

Cut the legs at the knuckle and pull the meat down to make a lollipop style with bone, stand up. Wrap the bone in foil. In a tray heat the fat with chilli and bay leaves, salt and pepper. Stand legs up in fat, loosely cover tray in foil to seal. Cook in the oven at 150°C for 45 minutes. Cool and dry the fat off with a cloth.

Remove meat from chicken legs and mix with flour, egg and breadcrumbs, then form into a ball round the base of the bone. Deep fry to finish. Fry breast until brown and reheat in oven for 10 minutes.

Creamed cabbage
Boil cabbage in chicken stock/butter/salt and pepper. Add mustard and cream, remove cabbage and reduce liquid by half. Return the cabbage to the pan.

Shallot and mushrooms
Fry the onions, mushrooms and tarragon. Add stock and reduce by a quarter. Add crème Fraiche and simmer for 3 minutes.

A VIEW TO DINE FOR

THERE'S a time and a place for technology in all sorts of businesses – but you must never lose touch with the basic skills.

Chris Marshall, chef director at Panoramic, knows all about it.

A hundred metres above street level, he reckons he has one of the best-equipped kitchens in Liverpool.

Then he corrects himself. "No, it's not probably, I know we have."

You want it, they've got it, be it a hi-tech Pacojet food processor or the temperature-controlled water baths for the sous vide method of cooking that can produce amazing and consistent results time after time in a busy kitchen. But Chris is adamant that he and his team must also know how to cook the traditional way.

"There wouldn't be any point in us using the technology or the techniques if, for example, we didn't know how to cook a piece of meat without it."

Chris himself is a native Liverpudlian from Speke who has followed in something of a family tradition, with a brother as a fellow chef and a sister a hotel general manager.

A spell at catering college in Widnes led to appointments up and down the country before he returned to his native North West.

From the kitchens at the Radisson hotel in Old Hall Street, it was a short step to take on Panoramic when it opened for business.

"It's been a good move," he reflects, "a fantastic location."

Panoramic highlight

RABBIT SADDLE WITH BOLOGNAISE AND ROASTED CARROTS

Here, Chris Marshall shares one of his favourite recipes from his last three years heading Panoramic's kitchen – rabbit saddle with bolognaise and roasted carrots. The usual rule of thumb is that one decent-sized rabbit will feed four people, and a good butcher will always joint and prepare the rabbit if asked.

Rabbit can be a somewhat dry meat – hence the need either to casserole it, or to wrap it in a fatty meat like bacon if cooking in an oven.

Remove all sinew from rabbit saddles. Roll the Parma ham tightly around the saddle to form a cylinder shape. Tie with kitchen string and chill in the fridge for about an hour. Heat the olive oil in a frying pan over a high heat and fry the rabbit for 3-4 minutes until browned on all sides. Transfer to the oven for 8-10 minutes or until cooked through. Remove from the oven and rest for 5 minutes. For the bolognaise, brown off the minced rabbit leg in hot oil and drain, then fry onions and 2 of the crushed garlic cloves together until soft, add the tomato puree and cook for 2 minutes. Pour in the port to glaze followed by the red wine and reduce by a half.

Add the bay leaf, thyme and 300ml of chicken stock and cook slowly for an hour and 50 minutes then finally add the demi-glaze and reduce until a deep colour is achieved. For the carrots, boil them with the remaining chicken stock and water, 1 crushed garlic clove, thyme, lemon zest and salt and pepper, until tender. Drain then rub in a cloth to remove the skin, rinse under water to make sure they are clean then place in a hot pan and cook until slightly caramelised. Slice the rabbit saddle and serve with the bolognaise, roasted carrots and a slice of pan-fried rabbit liver and kidney.

Serves 4
2 rabbit saddles
Parma ham
500g minced rabbit leg
Half a finely diced onion
3 garlic cloves
Tomato puree
100ml port
200ml red wine
1 bay leaf
Thyme
350ml brown chicken stock
500ml demi-glaze
Baby carrots
Lemon zest
Salt and pepper

welcome

LETS
COOK!

LET'S GET COOKING!

IF your experience of Chinese or Indian cuisine is limited to a gloopy dish served up in a foil takeaway container, then it's time for a culinary revolution.

Cue the expertise of the Can Cook Studios, who are calling on people to roll up their sleeves and get back in the kitchen.

Based at The Matchworks in Speke, Can Cook is a 20-place professional cookery school suitable for beginners as well as those who already enjoy cooking. Can Cook runs a number of courses in the evenings and at weekends, providing introductions to cuisines from around the world. Every course involves live demonstrations from skilled chefs and plenty of time for attendees to cook their own dishes in a state-of-the-art kitchen environment.

Robbie Davison, director of Can Cook Studios says: "We love teaching people how to cook their favourite foods in the studio and provide them with the skills to make these dishes and more in their kitchens at home. Can Cook want to get everybody involved in Liverpool's cooking revolution to get back to basics and get people back into the kitchen, creating old favourites and experimenting with delicious new dishes."

Forget dashing down to your local Indian restaurant on a Friday night or scanning the telephone directory for the fastest dial-a-pizza in town. Can Cook has provided three recipes here which are simple, delicious and cheap to make.

Robbie adds: "Recipes like this give you the chance to create a takeaway experience at home – cooking for the whole family, friends or just for you – with a healthier twist. But don't worry, healthier doesn't mean bland at Can Cook, as we aim to tread the line between making sure everything tastes great while being as healthy as we can make it."

Well then, let's get cooking!

For more information on the Can Cook Studios visit **www.cancookwillcook.org.uk**

PORK VINDALOO

Pork Vindaloo is a curry-house classic with a kick that has made it a favourite takeaway dish of us Brits for years.

Robbie Davison, Director of Can Cook Studios says: "This is a beautiful dish that is so simple to make and it's something that you can really impress your friends with. It's perfect served with plain basmati or pilau rice and a piece of nice, warm naan bread. You won't be able to get rid of your mates after this one!"

Serves 2

For the marinade
700g pork leg, diced to about 2.5cm
1 tsp ground cumin
4 cardamons, crushed
¼ tsp ground cloves
¼ tsp ground cinnamon
1 long red chilli, finely diced
1 birds eye chilli, finely diced
5cm piece of ginger, grated
4 cloves of garlic, crushed
3 tbsp lemon juice

For the curry
4 tbsp sunflower oil
5 cloves garlic, sliced
2 small onions, finely diced
1 tsp turmeric, ½ tsp chilli powder
½ tbsp tomato puree
3 tomatoes, chopped
3 tbsp white wine vinegar
10 curry leaves, salt to taste
4 tbsp fresh coriander, chopped

Put all of the ingredients for the marinade into a large bowl and mix well; cover and leave for at least an hour. Heat the oil in a pan and fry the onions and garlic over a medium heat for abut 5 minutes until the garlic is golden and the onions are soft. Add the turmeric, chilli powder, pork and marinade and cook for 2 minutes.

Now add the tomato puree, chopped tomatoes, vinegar and curry leaves and cook on a low heat with the lid on for about 60-90 minutes until the meat is very tender.

Add the chopped coriander and season with salt; serve with plain basmati rice or pilau rice.

Pork vindaloo

Nasi goreng

Prawn chow mein

NASI GORENG

Literally meaning 'fried rice' in Indonesian and Malay, this is a really simple supper dish with plenty of flavour. You can also serve this with a fried egg on top, intead of the omelette.

Serves 2
2 eggs, beaten
2 red chillies, seeded and shredded
1 onion, finely sliced
1 garlic clove, finely chopped
1 carrot, grated
150g sliced chestnut mushrooms
200g uncooked basmati rice
2 tbsp soft brown sugar
1 tbsp soy sauce
1 tbsp chilli sauce
¼ cucumber, finely sliced
A drizzle of sesame oil

Cook the rice as per the packet instructions. Fry the eggs into an omelette and slice into shreds once cooked. Set aside.

Heat the oil in a pan on medium heat. Add the onion, chilli, garlic, carrot and mushrooms and fry for 4 minutes. Add the cooked rice.

Mix together the sugar, soy sauce and chilli sauce and then add to the rice mix. Divide into 2 bowls. Add the sliced cucumber, shredded omelette and drizzle with sesame oil to serve.

PRAWN CHOW MEIN

Can Cook Studio's Prawn Chow Mein is a delicious recipe taught at their Chinese cooking classes. This is an amazing dish that you can make at home to save both the money and calories that come from the Friday night trip to the takeaway.

Serves 2
250g large peeled raw prawns
225g dried egg noodles
3 tbsp sunflower oil
1 yellow pepper, deseeded and sliced
100g button mushrooms, sliced
6 spring onions, shredded
100g beansprouts
2 cloves garlic, crushed
2 tsp grated ginger
2 tbsp light soy sauce
1 tbsp oyster sauce
½ tsp Chinese five spice
2 tbsp rice wine or sherry
2 tsp cornflour mixed with 2 tbsp water

Bring a large pan of water to the boil and cook the egg noodles as stated on the packet (usually about 4-5 minutes for medium egg noodles). Put the pan into an empty sink and allow cold water to run over the noodles to cool, then drain and set aside.

Heat a large frying pan with the sunflower oil until very hot; add the pepper, mushrooms, ginger and garlic and stir fry for 2 minutes. Add the prawns and continue to cook for 1 minute. Finally, add the beansprouts, noodles, oyster sauce, soy and five spice and continue to cook for 1 minute.

Add the rice wine and cornflour mix, stir in the spring onions and serve.

Ian Jaundoo, chef lecturer at Liverpool Community College

Chef Neil Dempsey

Tom Lee, Young Merseyside Chef of the Year 2010

TEACHING TOMORROW'S STARS

WHEN Ian Jaundoo dines at 60 Hope Street, chef Gary Manning makes sure the vegetables are julienned to just the right length.

Award-winning Gary - along with most of Merseyside's top chefs - learned his skills under Ian's watchful eye. In 27 years of teaching at Liverpool Community College's Academy restaurant he's nurtured the talents of Neil Dempsey, Gary Valentine and Tom Lee, junior sous chef at the London Carriage Works and Young Merseyside Chef of the Year 2010.

But Ian is as full of praise for dishes whisked up by current students, as those by its famous alumni. "They're tomorrow's stars," he explains.

Toxteth-born Ian, is of Trinidadian extraction. Food naturally plays a large part in West Indian culture and it's one that embraces lively flavours.

"Everything is based on the family sitting down to dinner, eating rice and peas, or chicken curry with roti," he explains. "So I guess I got the interest from there."

Ian, a Craft Guild of Chefs member for over 20 years, has won several awards and taken part in many competitions, nominated recently for Education Chef of the Year 2010.

He was asked to be a Craft Guild judge several years ago as well as the North West Guild representative. As culinary team manager at Liverpool Community College, Ian has concentrated on continually raising his skill levels - something he says is very important for all chefs - with salon culinaire competitions and travelling to the country's finest restaurants to learn new techniques.

Hungry for more at Academy

SCALLOPS ON BLACK PUDDING

Ian Jaundoo's final year NVQ Level 3 chefs provide a fine dining experience every Wednesday at Liverpool Community College's Academy restaurant on Duke Street.

"A lot of people see chefs on TV and it looks glamorous," he explains. "It can be but you have to work hard. To be a good chef you need passion about food, not just eating but knowing where it's come from and trying new types.

Dishes from the bistro and tasting menus are a fraction of restaurant prices. Ian says: "I think people would be very impressed at the quality on offer."

This recipe is from student Brian Riley. Check out The Academy menu at www.liv-coll.ac.uk.

Serves 2
6 king scallops
6 small discs of black pudding
100g garden peas
100g unsalted butter
150g mashed potato
100g leek
Half a sliced shallot
100ml shellfish bisque
50ml double cream
50ml fish stock
50ml vermouth
Olive oil
Salt and pepper

Season and prepare the potato to six small galettes. Cook the peas in the minimum of salted water, drain and blend to a puree, season, add butter and keep warm.

Prepare the sauce by reducing the vermouth and stock with shallot to half amount. Add the cream and bisque. Prepare the leek to julienne and blanch and butter glaze at service. Sauté the galettes and black pudding. Warm the puree and sauté the scallops separately.

To assemble, place three galettes on a plate and top with three discs of pudding; add the puree and scallops and mask with sauce; finish with leek garnish.

Giant German sausages at the
Williamson Square Continental Market

Lark Lane Farmer's Market

Buy your Kippers Here Today only £2·50 a Pair or 3 Pairs for £6·00 ready Now

Philip Taylor selling fresh kippers from the smoke box at Wirral Food and Drink Festival

Balsamic Mushrooms

Food for thought – Liverpool Food and Drink Festival and Hope Street Feast attract large crowds every year

Candice Fonseca

THE DELIFONSECA MOTTO - NO TOWERS OR DRIZZLES!

FOUNDED in 2006 by passionate foodie Candice Fonseca, Delifonseca focuses on flavour, variety and friendly service.

Candice says it was desperation for a good deli in Liverpool that led her to quit her old career, spend all her savings, and open the Stanley Street venture. She certainly made a smart move when bringing in Martin Cooper as head chef, who has spent more than 20 years at the forefront of Liverpool's dining scene. The food speaks for itself – Martin's motto is strictly "no towers or drizzles".

Delifonseca combines the best deli offerings with an excellent restaurant, and has picked up a hefty selection of awards, including 'Taste of Liverpool' in the Merseyside Tourism Awards 2009, 'SME Food Business of the Year' in the Food North West Awards 2009, along with the title of 'Restaurant of Excellence' at the Liverpool Food & Drink Festival Awards 2009. Head chef Martin Cooper and waiter Tom Ford also scooped awards at the Academy Ambassador Awards 2009.

With regular themed monthly wine tastings, as well as a bespoke hamper and outside catering service, there's very little they don't do. The team can source hard-to-find products and often add specialist selections such as edible flower petals to the ever-expanding product range.

Delifonseca focuses on rustic-style food. Good hearty meat stews and soups frequent the menu alongside fresh fish and vegetarian dishes. Salads and sandwiches accompany cheese platters and wraps on the menu, while the dessert selection on the blackboard rotates continually, so you're spoilt for choice. The motivation behind the menu is well cooked, seasonal produce, sourced as locally as possible.

Candice says: "We source quite a lot of our ingredients and stock for the restaurant from local companies, including Wirral, Aigburth and Kirkby. Our bread and milk is from Liverpool suppliers. When it comes to what we sell in the deli, produce can come from all around the globe.

"Our menu changes every day, depending on which products are in season and the mood of the chefs.

"Because we love food (and our customers) so much, we thought we'd share these recipes, so you can have a taste of Delifonseca at home, whenever you like!"

Deli-cious
MUFFULETA

The muffuleta is a classic New Orleans 'Italian' sandwich made in a special muffuleta loaf which is round and in a similar style to a soft focaccia. With these loaves being difficult to source in the UK, Delifonseca make their own rosemary focaccia buns daily, which complement the complex Mediterranean flavours of this sandwich.

Chef's note: the olive salad from this recipe keeps very well in the refrigerator and makes a wonderful addition to all kinds of salads and sandwiches!

Makes 6

The Bread
250g strong white flour
250g semolina flour (plus extra for dusting)
25g fresh yeast
400ml warm water at 37°C
2 tbsp olive oil (plus extra for drizzling)
1 tsp salt
Half tsp caster sugar
2 tbsp dried rosemary

Olive Salad
300g mixed pitted olives (in oil)
4-5 pickled pimento peppers
200g sunblushed tomatoes
2 tbsp olive oil
2 cloves of garlic
3 tsp dried oregano
100g fresh parsley

The Sandwich
300g Serrano Ham
300g Milano Salami
300g Comte (thinly sliced)

Pre-heat the oven to 210°C/Gas Mark 6. Begin by making the focaccia buns. Crumble the yeast and sugar into the warm water (37°C). Leave for 10-15 minutes stirring regularly. Place the flours into a large bowl, along with the salt, a good splash of olive oil and the yeast mixture. Knead quickly in the bowl to form a batter-like dough, adding more oil so the dough doesn't form a crust. Cover the bowl with a clean tea towel and leave in a warm place to prove for an hour.

In the meantime, make the olive salad by placing all the listed ingredients into a food processor along with the extra olive oil from the pitted olives. Blend until a coarse tapenade is formed. Flour your hands with some of the semolina flour and divide the bread dough into 6 pieces. Knead these pieces into round, quite flat buns.

With the end of a wooden spoon, place a few holes into the top of each bun. Place these on a well oiled baking tray. Drizzle the buns with a little more olive oil and sprinkle on the rosemary. Leave these to rise for a further half an hour to double in size.
Bake for 20 minutes or until golden brown.

Once the bread has cooled down, it's time to construct your sandwich! Slice your buns in half horizontally and spread the top and bottom of the bread with the olive salad (to taste). Place the salami, then the cheese, then ham on top of one another and heat in the oven until the cheese starts to melt – delicious!

Come Dine With Me winner
Ian Cook at Studio2;
opposite page, best friends
Ian and Niki O'Leary enjoy
the vegan breakfast

'TELEVISION SHOW THAT CHANGED MY LIFE'

CHANNEL 4's Come Dine With Me has whetted people's appetites for discovering their inner chef and entertaining at home.

Leading from the front in Liverpool is the aptly-named Ian Cook. He is the former BT customer services manager, from Allerton, who collected the £1,000 prize in 2006.

From entertaining just four people round his table, he's gone on to feeding up to 70 people at a time - after he chucked in his job and began a new life as a chef.

"Before Come Dine With Me, I didn't really realise how good I was", says Ian. "It gave me the confidence to make some key decisions."

First was to quit work as a customer services manager.

"I went to work in Spain for 18 months, learning the language and the cuisine.

"When I came back, I thought, I don't want to go back to what I was doing before. I thought about going back to college and doing it that way but a friend put me in touch with Cameron Acott, at Parr Street Studios, who offered me a place in the kitchen at Studio2."

Come Dine With Me was the real turning point for Ian. His TV guests were vegan Niki O'Leary, fishmonger Dan Redfern and traditionalist

Margaret Twemlow, who served her seafood starter on the beach in West Kirby.

"My meal was very, very simple and based around the fact Niki was a vegan, so I did roasted butternut squash and red lentil soup with garlic croutons, followed by whole roasted seabass with tartar potato cake and parsley and cream sauce.

"For Niki, I did roasted tofu with a tomato reduction. I wanted to be as inclusive as possible and make less work for me."

Niki is now one of Ian's best friends. She runs the ScouseVeg social group and website for vegetarians and vegans in Merseyside, and often drops into Studio2 to sample Ian's critically-acclaimed vegan breakfast. With no animal products in it at all, the vegan option boasts vegan bacon, vegan sausages, griddled potato, grilled tomato and mushroom, and Heinz baked beans.

Ian says: "I buy the vegan produce from Matta's International Foods on Bold Street. The quality and portions are just as good as the full English and vegetarian breakfast, so it's good value for money.

"Our vegan breakfast is quite unique and there really are not many places that do it.

"One customer from Leeds burst into tears when he ate it - he said it was the best vegan breakfast he'd ever tasted!"

The secret House
MOROCCAN VEGETABLE TAGINE

Serves 4

1 red onion
1 yellow pepper
1 red pepper
1 courgette
8/10 mushrooms
1 aubergine
1 carrot, parboiled
1 sweet potato
Small tin of chick peas
1 small tin chopped tomatoes
150ml vegetable stock
Honey, salt and pepper to taste
Fresh coriander and flat leaf parsley

Tagine Paste

Ground coriander, ginger, turmeric
smoked paprika, cumin seeds
ground cumin, 2 cloves of garlic

Tucked away from the hustle and bustle of Hope Street, the award winning Blackburne House Café Bar is a real hidden gem. With a relaxed ambience and bright, airy and welcoming surroundings, it's perfect for a pre-theatre stop or a relaxed evening, spent chatting and enjoying a glass of wine with friends.

The Café Bar is renowned for its excellent selection of international and vegetarian dishes all prepared in house using the finest locally sourced ingredients.

Chef Claire Southern says: "This is an authentic Moroccan recipe that we serve in our café bar. It proves popular with our vegetarian customers and is a healthy nutritious meal that's not too spicy. The dish can be made vegan if you substitute the honey for sugar. The cous cous can be made by adding lemon zest and juice, butter and toasted pine nuts, fresh herbs, chopped dried apricots and sultanas to the basic mix."

Make the tagine paste by mixing 1 teaspoon of each of the dried spices with the crushed garlic and a tablespoon of olive oil. Chop all vegetables into a medium dice. Add to a pan with the tagine paste. Fry on a low heat for 4/5 minutes. Add tin of chopped tomatoes and 150ml vegetable stock.

Simmer for 5 minutes and add a squeeze of honey along with the chopped herbs. Add the drained chick peas. Season and serve with warm cous cous.

Ahead of its time
SALMON, LEEK AND SPINACH ROSTI BAKE

Claire Southern, chef at Blackburne House Café Bar, says: "This is a wonderful dish that can be prepared in advance. Best to be served with fine green beans and baby carrots."

Serves 4
4 salmon fillets, skinned
1 large leek
1 bag of baby spinach
200ml double cream
100ml vegetable stock
4 large potatoes
Salt and pepper
100g melted butter

Peel the potatoes and parboil whole in salted water for 10 minutes. Drain and cool.

Meanwhile, slice the raw salmon into thin slivers and put half on the base of a greased baking dish. Sauté the sliced washed leeks in a small amount of butter and season with salt and pepper. When the leeks are softened, add the washed and drained spinach into the pan, and allow it to wilt for a minute.

Place half the spinach mixture on top of the salmon, then arrange the rest of the salmon on top of that, finish with the remaining spinach mixture. Next, mix the cream and stock together and pour over the salmon.

Finally, grate the potatoes over the top, season and finish by drizzling melted butter over the top. Bake for 30 minutes on 170°C until golden.

St John's beacon

LEMON ALMOND DRIZZLE CAKE

Since joining Rapid's Signature Café, head chef Stewart St John is keen to provide good wholesome food from scratch without breaking the bank.

Stewart says: "I love the challenge of providing good, fresh, traditional food, taking it up market but retaining cafe prices."

Makes a 10 inch cake
250g butter room temp, 250g sugar, 250g eggs, 250g flour, 15g baking powder, 2 lemons, vanilla essence

For the drizzle
Juice of 2 lemons, 30g clear honey, 25g sugar, vanilla essence, 1 tsp coriander seed

Cream the butter, sugar and vanilla. Add the eggs gradually. Add the flour, almonds, baking powder and lemon zest – cream until smooth. Bake at 140°C for 45 minutes.

For the drizzle, boil all the ingredients until a light syrup, sieve and cool. When the cake is baked, remove from the oven and prick with a skewer. Drizzle with syrup, but not too much as the cake will go stodgy.

An all-star breakfast

BLACK PUDDING WITH SMOKED HADDOCK AND HOLLANDAISE

Leon Yeadon, head chef at the Little Green Café Bar on Aigburth Road, is a firm believer in the importance of a good breakfast. A multi-talented chef, Leon has over 29 years of experience in the industry and has cooked for some of music's biggest stars on tour.

Here, he shares his culinary secrets and shows you how to cook up a great breakfast with one of his favourite dishes – black pudding with smoked haddock and hollandaise sauce.

Melt the butter and nutmeg in a frying pan and cook the spinach until wilted. Next, grill the four slices of black pudding for around two minutes on each side and poach the smoked haddock over a medium heat for around one minute or until heated through.

Serves 4
Four slices of black pudding
One piece of smoked haddock
One medium bag of fresh spinach
A knob of butter
A pinch of nutmeg

For the Hollandaise:
2 egg yolks
A sprig of fresh tarragon
One tbsp of white wine vinegar
8oz of butter

For the sauce, place a heat proof bowl over a pan of boiling water and add the white wine vinegar, before whisking in the two egg yolks and a table spoon of cold water. In a separate pan, melt the butter and slowly add to the sauce mixture while whisking until it reaches a smooth consistency and finish by sprinkling in the chopped tarragon. To serve, place a generous amount of spinach on each plate, topped with two slices of black pudding and half of the smoked haddock fillet (per portion) and garnish with your homemade Hollandaise sauce.

A wonder of Wirral

SPICY LAMB SOUP (ARABIAN SHERBA)

Tucked away in the town of Hoylake, Julian's Restaurant is one of Wirral's best kept secrets.

Since it launched in 2004, the restaurant has built up a reputation for offering the best in fine dining. Making the most of what is in season and using only the best, locally sourced ingredients, the menu is Mediterranean in style with a British twist.

Serves 4

1 dessertspoon black pepper
1 dessertspoon chilli flakes
2 tbsp mint sauce
1 cup of olive oil
1 chopped onion
2 mixed peppers
1 courgette
Half bulb of garlic
500g finely diced lamb
1 large tin of chopped tomatoes
1 dessertspoon of sugar
15-20 strands of dried spaghetti
2.5 litres of chicken stock

Heat the oil in a deep pan and add the chopped onion, diced peppers and courgette, and sauté for 5 minutes. Add the black pepper, chili flakes, garlic and mint sauce and mix together.

Put the diced lamb into the pan and mix until all the meat is sealed. Pour in the tinned tomatoes with the sugar and chicken stock. Bring to the boil and add the spaghetti, broken into half inch pieces. Continue to boil for another 20 minutes. Leave to cool.

You can serve the soup straight away if you wish, but it tastes even better if it's left overnight and reheated the next day.

Something a bit different
CHICKEN ROULADE

Julian Davies, proprietor and chef of Julian's Restaurant, brings his own unique cooking style to the table and has combined his love of international travel, his classical French training and his passion for fresh British ingredients, to create an ever-changing and eclectic menu.

Serves 4
1 fresh chicken breast
50g leaf spinach
20g tomato concasse
Half a pint of whipping cream
Half a cup of tomato juice
Seasoning
Fresh tarragon to taste
Half a cup of white wine

Flatten the chicken breast gently so as not to tear the flesh. Place the blanched spinach and a spoonful of the tomato concasse onto the chicken. Roll in cling film and wrap it up and twist both ends to seal.

Boil in water for approximately 15-20 minutes.

To make the sauce, reduce the white wine, cream and seasoning. Then add the tarragon and tomato juice.

Remove the cling film from the chicken and slice into 4 or 5 pieces and serve immediately with the sauce drizzled over.

Child's play at Gusto

JELLY AND ICE-CREAM

As childhood desserts go, they don't come much simpler or better loved than jelly and ice cream.

Graham Kirk, executive chef at Gusto, says: "It is always a popular dish on the menu at Gusto and we think you would be hard pushed to find a child who wouldn't love this."

Serves 2
4 leaves gelatine
8oz fresh berries
300ml fresh berry juice (cranberry or mixed berry)
2 sprigs mint
2 scoops vanilla ice cream

Place the berries and the juice into a pan and bring to the boil. Simmer gently for 4-5 minutes until the berries are soft.

Pass the mixture through a sieve to remove any skins and seeds. Soak the gelatine leaves in cold water for 3-4 minutes, until softened. Squeeze the excess water from the gelatine and add to the berry liquid and stir until fully dissolved.
Pour the mixture into moulds or glasses, and chill in the fridge for 3-4 hours until set.

To Serve
Turn the jelly onto a serving plate. Place one or two scoops of the ice cream beside each jelly and garnish with the mint sprig.
Dust with icing sugar if desired, and serve.

PRAWNS IN A GARLIC, TOMATO AND CREAM SAUCE

If your little ones are scared off by fish, covering it in sauce is a good move. This prawn dish is easy and tasty.

Serves 2
16 prawns
2 cloves of garlic
Fresh parsley (small bunch)
500ml double cream
1 jar of tomato sauce
Salt
Pepper
Olive oil
Fresh basil

Heat your pan up on a moderate heat, add 4tbsp of olive oil. Sweat your prawns in the olive oil adding the garlic, cook on both sides to ensure they are fully cooked (3 mins each side).

Season the prawns slightly with salt and pepper and add half of the jar of tomato sauce and half of the cream.

Cook the sauce on a gentle heat (be careful not to burn) and season to taste.

Place eight prawns into each dish, adding the sauce on top and garnish with fresh basil.

APPLE, WALNUT & GORGONZOLA SALAD

Looking for a simple but tasty dish that everyone will enjoy? Then this salad is for you. Gorgonzola isn't too strong a cheese and most children will eat apples.

Serves 2
Small bag of baby spinach
1 red apple
Gorgonzola cheese
1 little gem lettuce
Chives
Honey
Walnuts
English mustard
1 lemon
Olive oil

Dice the apple, removing the seeds and wash the salad leaves.

To make the salad dressing, mix together the juice and zest of one lemon with half a teaspoon of English mustard, one teaspoon of olive oil and a pinch of salt and pepper.

Place all of the ingredients into a bowl mixing in your salad dressing. Scatter the walnuts and diced cheese over your salad.

Drizzle with honey and garnish with chives before serving.

Quick and wholesome

PENNE PASTA WITH TOMATO SAUCE

This penne pasta dish with tomato sauce is very quick and simple to make, which means youngsters won't lose concentration during the preparation. Despite its simplicity, this dish is wholesome and filling and is very popular on the Gusto menu.

Serves 2
1 jar tomato sauce for pasta
Half an onion
150g dried penne pasta
1 dessert spoon chopped parsley
50g parmesan cheese, finely grated
2 dessert spoons olive oil
2 cloves garlic
Salt and pepper

Finely chop the onion, add to a saucepan along with one dessert spoon of olive oil and gently sweat. Bring a pan of water to the boil and add rest of olive oil. Place pasta in the water and cook following packet instructions. Add tomato sauce to the onion and mix together thoroughly.

When pasta is cooked, drain and shake to remove excess water, add the parmesan and parsley to the sauce and mix in the pasta. Season to taste with salt and pepper and divide between two bowls.

Top with more parmesan if desired.

ANT & BAR

Summer IN THE CITY

SURELY the best thing about a heatwave is being able to soak up the rays and enjoy some refreshing drinks and dinner in the great outdoors?

Whether you fancy a refreshing pint of real ale after work or a relax with a jug of sangria on a summery Sunday afternoon, there are lots of places in Liverpool, from traditional beer gardens complete with picnic tables and hanging baskets to continental style eateries and trendy roof terraces.

When the sun starts cracking the flags, you can enjoy outdoor eating at the Albert Dock, Liverpool ONE, Concert Square – the world is your oyster . . . or sushi roll, or fajita . . .

171

NEW LIFE BESIDE THE SEASIDE

THE Red Door neighbourhood bar and kitchen opened in West Kirby in April 2010.

The former funeral parlour on Grange Road, bought by entrepreneurs Tim Bacon and David Hinds in 2009, has been transformed into a stylish bar.

An extensive wine and cocktail menu, is complimented by a food menu which has been designed for sharing. A selection of small plates served tapas style runs alongside top-quality burgers and sandwiches. The chilled vibe from this cool neighbourhood bar and kitchen is a welcome addition to the seaside town of West Kirby.

In this recipe, chef Mark Johnson gives us a real taste of summer with burgers, perfect for a barbecue.

Mark says: "You can buy your burgers from the butchers but, without doubt, the best burgers are homemade.

"Ask your butcher for some well-trimmed chuck steak, and ask him to mince it twice on a medium-sized mincing plate.

"When you get home, chill the meat for one hour."

Barbecue best

Red Door chef Mark Johnson says: "Burgers are best cooked on a chargrill or barbecue. Allow the burger to cook at its own pace, don't squash it down. The salsa is best made 24 hours in advance so the wonderful flavours can infuse."

CLASSIC BURGER WITH TOMATO & CORIANDER SALSA

Serves 4
For the burger
500g beef burger chuck
1 white onion
Salt and pepper

For the tomato and coriander salsa
8 ripe vine tomatoes
1 medium white onion
1 yellow pepper
Half fresh red chilli
1 clove garlic
50g chopped fresh coriander
2 tbsp extra virgin olive oil
100ml pasata (optional)
Salt and pepper to taste

To serve
4 floured baps
1 little gem lettuce
2 tomatoes, sliced
1 red onion, sliced
4 dill pickles
Salt and pepper

For the Salsa
Remove the core of the tomatoes and cut in half. Remove all of the seeds, then dice into 1/2cm pieces. Put into the mixing bowl. Peel the onion and dice into 1/2cm pieces. Cut the peppers in half lengthways and remove the seeds and stalk. Bang the pepper open side into your hand to remove any stubborn seeds. Dice into the same size as the onion. Roughly chop the coriander and finely chop the chilli. Place the onion, pepper, chilli, coriander, extra virgin olive oil, salt and pepper into the bowl with the tomatoes and combine evenly. Add the pasata. Place in the fridge to chill.

For the Burgers
Finely dice the white onion, remove the chilled meat from the fridge and add the onion, season with salt and pepper. Mix together and then divide into 4 even amounts. Mould the burgers with your hands into round and flat patties, return to the fridge for 20 minutes. Heat the bbq, grill, griddle or pan so it is smoking. Lightly oil the burger and place onto the char-grill for 2 minutes, then turn over. Cook for a further 2 minutes, then turn back over and cook for 1 minute, turn again and cook for another minute. This should give you a medium burger. If you are using a frying pan, griddle or grill, this may take longer – approximately 5-6 minutes each side. Cut the baps through the centre and open out, char on both sides. Serve the burger in the bap with the lettuce, sliced tomato, dill pickle and onion. Skewer through the whole thing but don't press down, the garnish is designed to give height.

BOHEMIAN HOT SPOT

A MEETING place all day long, The Quarter's unique atmosphere attracts a variety of guests from businessmen to bohemians.

Head chef Andrew Mountfield prides himself on using the best, fresh, seasonal produce and creating delicious dishes. Located on Falkner Street in the city's cultural quarter, The Quarter keeps it simple with pizzas, pastas, salads and a delectable selection of daily specials.

Andrew says: "We keep our customers happy by using the best quality, fresh, local produce to create their all time favourite dishes as well as some intriguing new specials. Our al fresco dining area is a much-loved hot spot in the summer months and there's nothing better than a relaxing evening here with a hearty bowl of pasta and a crisp glass of white wine."

Strawberry Cupcake £14.50

From the sea to the patio

SOUTHPORT SHRIMP FETTUCCINE

Andrew Mountfield, head chef at The Quarter, says: "Southport Shrimp fettuccine is quick and easy to make, perfect for those warm summer evenings when you want to get out of the kitchen and on to the patio to enjoy yourself. Made with delicious seasonal Claremont Farm asparagus and award winning Southport potted shrimps, this dish couldn't get any more local. Enjoy!"

Serves 4
350g fettuccine or pasta
110g Southport Potted Shrimp (one tub)
150g Claremont Farm asparagus - thinly sliced on an angle
100g Wirral rocket
80g grated parmesan cheese
100g crème fraiche
Salt and pepper

Cook the pasta as per instructions in boiling salted water. The asparagus can be cooked in with the pasta for 3-5 minutes depending on the size of the stalks, do not overcook, asparagus should still be al dente. In a separate pan melt and warm the shrimps through on a low heat, releasing all the spices and flavours.

When the pasta and asparagus are cooked, drain and return to the pan and add melted butter and shrimp. Add grated parmesan, crème fraiche and rocket. Fold in gently and allow the rocket to wilt slightly. Season, toss and serve, with a crisp glass of sauvignon blanc or a Hawkshead beer.

PASSION AND HOPE

DAMIEN Flynn, head chef 60 Hope Street, has a love of seafood that is continually built into the fresh, seasonal menu he and his team have created within this fine dining establishment in Liverpool's Cultural Quarter.

Damien says: "There are too many people that avoid cooking shellfish such as lobster and prawns because they believe they are difficult to prepare and cook correctly. This is a dish that anyone can produce well with a little bit of time and care in the kitchen and the lobster can even be grilled on the barbeque when the weather warms up – delicious!"

60 Hope Street is one of Liverpool's most beloved eateries and is run by two local brothers, Colin and Gary Manning.

Along with an unrivalled international experience and the knowledge of running a family run business, the one element that remains at the heart of 60 Hope Street is the passion for great food and that really shows in the dishes that Damien and his team create.

Dressed to impress

LOBSTER AND PRAWN SALAD

Damien Flynn says: "This lobster and prawn salad is a perfect dish for the warmer summer months and something that will certainly impress your dinner guests."

Serves 2
2 x lobsters 1 - 1 ½ lb live
1lb fresh water prawns
4 carrots diced
¼ celery roughly chopped
3 bay leaves
1 onion diced
1 lemon
Salt & peppercorns

In a large pan, three quarters full of water, add plenty of salt, chopped vegetables, bay leaves, lemon juice and the used lemon. Bring to boil and simmer for 5 minutes.

Add the lobsters then increase the heat to bring to a vigorous boil. Cook on a rolling boil for approximately 8-10 minutes depending on weight – lobster should float when cooked. Remove and rest to allow it to cook in its shell and avoid under cooking. Allow time to cool and chill if required.

To prepare, remove claws at the elbow and using the back of a cook's knife split the claws. Cut the lobster in half lengthways, head first between the eyes and cut down through the tail. Remove the feathery gills, green liver and stomach and carefully pull out dark intestinal tract along tail. Fill the head cavity with fresh water prawns. Serve with a crisp, green salad and new potatoes.

Tip: Lobster can also be cut live and grilled on the barbecue with garlic or chilli butter.

ATOMIC KITCHEN FOR MASTERCHEF WINNER

WHEN singer Liz McClarnon entered Celebrity Masterchef, she had never even used an oven.

But she soon proved to be a real talent in the kitchen, and fought off stiff competition to win the cooking crown of the BBC1 series in 2008.

Throughout the final stages, Liz's cooking abilities were tested to the limit as she joined Toxteth-born actor Mark Moraghan and presenter Andi Peters to cook for 600 builders, army cadets in the field and Michelin-starred chefs, including Michel Roux Jr.

Liz puts her success down to inspiration from her mum, Janet.

"My mum is the best cook ever. She can make anything and she loves cookery programmes. So, when Celebrity Masterchef came up she made me do it. I said 'I'm not going to get very far' but she said I had to do it, so I agreed. You can't say no to my mum. She won't have it."

Liz was joined on the show by fellow Scousers Mark Moraghan, Joe McGann and Louis Emerick.

"We had a great solidarity," laughs Liz. "We got on really well. You always get that thing where you meet another Scouser when you're in London or wherever and you have an instant bond. Well we had that times four."

Since winning Celebrity Masterchef, Liz has taught easy-to-follow recipes on GMTV's LK Today and had a regular spot on UKTV'S Market Kitchen. She is also cooking up a storm on her website, with a foodie section offering some of her favourite recipes, as well as videos with demonstrations of some quick and easy dishes.

Liz says she is going back to basics: "The first time I tried to make batter on Masterchef I didn't know which oil I needed to use, I was really confused.

"I want to take things right back to basics and teach people how to boil an egg or make the perfect mashed potato."

"My website is really popular and I thought it would be a fun element to the site."

For more of Liz's recipes go to **www.lizmcclarnon.com**

Back to basics

SEABASS WITH WATERCRESS SALSA

Serves 2
4 small sea bass fillets, a little oil for brushing

For the salsa
1 red chilli, deseeded and chopped, 1 tbsp capers, drained, 2 spring onions trimmed, 1 x 85g bag watercress, 2 tbsp olive oil, juice of half a lemon, Salt and freshly ground black pepper

To serve
New potatoes and watercress

Brush the fish fillets on both sides with a little oil and season to taste. Place skin side down on a foil lined grill rack and cook under a hot grill for 6-8 mins or until cooked through. Meanwhile, place all the salsa ingredients together in a food processor and whizz on the pulse setting until a smooth sauce has formed. Season to taste and spoon into a serving bowl. To serve, take four plates, arrange a little watercress on each and place the fish on top. Spoon the salsa over the fish and serve with new potatoes.

Keeping it simple

LEMON SOLE

Graham Kirk, executive chef at Gusto, believes in using fresh, seasonal ingredients and treating the products with the respect they deserve. "Don't over-complicate flavours – I like to let the main ingredient do the talking," he says.

"That's why I choose dishes which demonstrate good quality, fresh ingredients with basic flavours. You can achieve from those a beautiful dish that makes the mouth water.

"I think this is a very visual, summer dish with the colours of the pesto and the lemon butter on the plate. The golden crumbs on top of the sole just add a little texture and the flavour of the green olive tapenade comes out beautifully after baking."

Serves 2

2 x 180g double fillets of lemon sole - ask your fishmonger to remove the skin, bones and the feathers
2 slices white bread - crusts removed
100ml tomato sauce, shop bought tomato sauce, soup or passata is fine
8 cherry tomatoes
20g baby spinach leaves
1 lemon
50g butter
1 dessert spoon double cream
1 dessert spoon pesto sauce
15 green olives
2 sprigs basil
1 tsp capers
2 dessert spoons olive oil
Black pepper

First make the tapenade – place the green olives and capers in a blender and pulse to achieve a chunky paste that is not completely smooth, add the basil and the olive oil and blend together. The mixture should be paste-like but still have little pieces of olive in it.

Season with black pepper and place in the fridge until required. Blend the bread slices to make fine breadcrumbs – place to the side until required.

Lay the lemon sole out flat (so that the side which would have had the skin on is facing upwards). Place one dessert spoon of the tapenade into the centre of the sole fillet and fold over to cover the tapenade. Sprinkle the fish with salt and breadcrumbs and place on a lightly oiled baking tray and into the oven set at 150-180°C. The fish will take 8-10 minutes to cook depending on thickness.
For the sauce, add the cream to a pan and squeeze the juice from the lemon into it – bring to the simmer and whisk in the butter, being careful not to allow the butter to boil or the sauce will split. When smooth and shiny, add a little salt and pepper and taste to ensure that there is a good lemon flavour.

To serve, heat the tomato sauce on the stove, cut the cherry tomatoes in half and add to the pan along with the spinach and mix thoroughly. Season with salt and pepper to taste. Spoon the tomato mix into the centre of the plates. Remove the fish from the oven (breadcrumbs should be golden brown) and place on top of the tomato mix. Drizzle a spoonful of the butter sauce around the fish and then a teaspoonful of the pesto.

Dockside delight

PAN-FRIED DUCK BREAST WITH PANCETTA

Having developed a strong and faithful following with Wirral's local fashionistas and discerning diners, the Liverpool Gusto opened its doors at the Albert Dock in 2008.

The Italian-inspired restaurant set in a former tobacco warehouse is now one of the most popular dock venues and has gained a reputation for superb food in lovely surroundings.

This duck with pancetta and a creamy leek sauce, is a wholesome main course – while light enough for summer too.

Executive chef Graham Kirk says: "I love duck and I adore this dish because of the smokiness of the pancetta combined with the creamy leeks. It's a wonderful combination."

Serves 2
2 duck breasts
2 small carrots
1 leek - white only
100g pancetta - smoked (streaky bacon would be fine)
60ml double cream
6 sprigs parsley, four of which should be chopped up
75ml red wine sauce

Score the skin of the duck through to the meat, 12-15 times at regular intervals along the breast to allow the fat to melt during cooking.

Remove the green top of the leek and cut down the centre, wash to remove any grit. Cut the leek into 5cm lengths and finely julienne into strips. Peel, top and tail the carrots and julienne. Mix the carrot and leek evenly together and blanch in boiling water for 2 minutes. Refresh in cold water and drain the water off.

Refresh the vegetables in cold water and allow to drain thoroughly. Season the duck on both sides with salt and pepper and place into a moderately hot frying pan – no oil will be required as the duck will release a lot of fat.

Cook gently on the skin side for five to six minutes – draining any excess fat from the pan wherever possible. Turn the duck breasts over and continue cooking for two to three minutes on the flesh side. Remove the duck from the pan and leave in a warm place to rest the meat. Drain any excess fat from the pan again and add the pancetta/bacon – fry until crisp – add the carrot and leeks and mix together thoroughly. Add the double cream to the pan and bring together to bind the mixture, then add the chopped parsley to this and season with salt and pepper (taste before adding the salt as the bacon/pancetta will be salty).

Heat up the red wine sauce. Slice the duck breast into five pieces each. Divide the carrot and leek mix between two serving plates and fan the carved duck around, drizzle the plates with the red wine sauce and garnish with the parsley sprig.

Comfort classic

SLOWLY BRAISED LAMB SHANK

In his seven years of working in the catering industry, Paul Fuller, head chef at The James Monro in Liverpool, has created everything from speciality desserts to gastro-pub classics such as rump steak and beer battered cod.

Paul says: "I have been lucky enough to work alongside some of the best chefs in the city, learning how to create dishes that diners will want to come back for time and time again. Now everyone calls me a young Heston Blumenthal because of the way I like to think outside of the recipe book and experiment with ingredients.

"This slowly braised lamb shank dish is a pure comfort food classic inspired by the irresistible home cooked food that I used to regularly enjoy as a child visiting my grandma. The addition of rosemary, thyme and mint to the dish also makes it a fantastic seasonal meal, while the red wine gives it an extra special twist that will appeal to all diners who are looking to spoil themselves and don't want to compromise on taste."

Serves 4
4 lamb shanks
Sea salt
Cracked black pepper
4 carrots (peeled and roughly chopped)
2 white onions (peeled and cut into quarters)
1 glass of good red wine
4 sprigs of thyme
20 mint leaves
Olive oil
4 sprigs of rosemary
1 whole bulb of garlic (cut lengthways)

Pre heat oven to 200°C. Rub lamb shanks all over with olive oil, salt and pepper and set aside.

Place the carrots, onions, herbs and garlic in a pan with a little oil and gently cook until just golden brown. Place into a deep tray or casserole dish and add the red wine. Place all shanks on top and cover tightly with tin foil and place in oven.

After one hour lower the temperature down to 160°C and leave to cook for about 2-3 hours or until the meat pulls away from the bone. It should be nice and sticky at this point.

Serve with buttery mash, red cabbage and gravy.

Everyman soul food

HAM, LEEK AND BUTTER BEAN SOUP

When it's wet, windy, cold and dark, the body needs food not only as nourishment, but as a psychological pick-me-up. Soul food, if you like.

Tom Gill, head chef at The Everyman Bistro says winter warmers are exactly his favourite kind of food. "This food season is one of my favourites, I much prefer hearty soup and broth dishes as they're always really satisfying to make for customers!" Here is one of Tom's recipes for you to try at home.

Serves 4
1 ham hock
200g butter beans
2 leeks sliced and washed
2 carrots diced
1 small onion finely chopped

For the stock
Rosemary
Thyme
1 carrot
Half an onion
1 celery stick

Soak the beans overnight. Drain off the water they have soaked in then cover with fresh unsalted water and boil until cooked, then drain and season with plenty of salt and pepper. Cover the ham hock and stock vegetables with cold water then bring to the boil, skim and simmer for two hours (covered). Remove the ham and allow to cool slightly then remove the meat from the bone.

Strain the stock and add 1500ml to a pan, then bring to the boil and add the carrots and onion. Simmer for five minutes then add the leeks, beans and ham, then continue simmering until the leeks are tender and serve with crusty bread.

TOFFEE, APPLE & CUSTARD BROWN BETTY

Brown Betty is the name given to a dessert when buttered crumbs are mixed with sugar and layered with fruit before baking. Pam Wellings of The Everyman Bistro says: "Feel free to add toasted nuts or cinnamon to your breadcrumbs. Either bake in individual ceramic pots or in a large ovenproof dish."

Serves 6

Breadcrumbs
7oz fresh breadcrumbs
3oz butter (melted)
4oz caster sugar

Apples
2lb cooking apples, peeled and cored
Extra caster sugar for taste

Toffee sauce
8oz golden syrup
8oz light brown sugar
2oz butter
Half a pint of double cream

Vanilla custard
4oz caster sugar
2oz cornflour
4 egg yolks
1 pint of milk
1 vanilla pod (split with seeds scraped out)

Toss the breadcrumbs with the melted butter and then mix in the sugar, then leave to one side. Cut the apples into chunks and toss with caster sugar depending on how sweet you want your apples. Place in a baking tray and cook in a pre-heated oven (180°C/gas mark 4) until just soft. Place the syrup, sugar and butter in a heavy bottomed pan and heat gently until all the ingredients are combined and the sugar has dissolved. Then boil rapidly on a higher heat for 2-3 minutes, carefully add the cream and stir until incorporated. Remove from the heat and leave to cool.

Beat together the egg yolks, cornflour and sugar in a large bowl and leave to one side. Add the vanilla to the milk and place in a heavy bottomed pan, then heat the milk to almost boiling point. Whisk all the ingredients together by pouring the milk into the egg, sugar mixture then pour everything back into the pan and stir until the custard thickens. Remove from the heat and leave to cool.
Once you have all four components ready and cooled it's time to assemble the dessert. Begin with the apple, followed by the toffee sauce then crumbs, then another layer of apple, followed by the custard, then top with the crumbs.

Bake in the oven (180°C/gas mark 4) for 15-20 minutes until the crumb topping is crisp and browned. Serve warm with cream or extra custard or just as it is – a complete dessert in one!

The perfect Christmas dinner

Cooking Christmas dinner can be quite a daunting task, but if you are worried about your sprouts going soggy or your rotten roasties, panic not – here, some of Liverpool's top chefs share their seasonal secrets. It's easy when you know how!

Christmas Gravy a la Vincent from The Vincent Hotel

Place your cooked turkey on the hob, and add oil, some diced onions and a carrot. Fry until golden, then add two leeks and one or two cloves of garlic and continue to fry until the vegetables have softened. Add a little flour to thicken and then deglaze the tray with a generous splash of red wine. Add one celery stick, diced, and the stock from your Christmas dinner vegetables, then add a sprig of thyme and sage and a pinch of salt – simmer for 15 minutes and pass through a sieve.

Perfect Brussel sprouts, The Living Room

To prevent Brussel sprouts from being soggy and to ensure they are evenly cooked, criss-cross the bottom of the core. For a festive twist, heat a pan with olive oil, add some pancetta and chopped chestnuts and sauté, cut the cooked sprouts in half and add to the pan. Season to taste and finish off with freshly chopped parsley.

Port and chestnut sauce, Malmaison

Simply sweat some shallots in a pan and add equal amounts of cooked chestnuts. Cover with a good Tawny Port and turn the heat down low to simmer until the chestnuts have broken down and all the port has been soaked in. Make sure it does not catch on the pan, if it is too dry add some more port. Pulse in the blender to marry the shallots with the chestnuts, add some picked thyme. This will add a real sweet and savoury appeal to your festive table.

Perfect turkey and roast potatoes, Gusto

Always use a probe to monitor cooking your turkey at 75°C. Glaze your turkey with honey and butter, and most importantly let it rest for 20 minutes before you carve.
For great roasties, par-boil potatoes, cut them into big pieces, give them a shake in a strainer to rough them up, then plunge them straight into hot dripping, goose fat or vegetable oil.

189

Sweet result

CHRISTMAS PUDDING & BRANDY BUTTER

Most of us tuck into a traditional Christmas pudding, which has origins dating back to the 1420s when it wasn't seen as a confection or a dessert, but as a way of preserving meat at the end of the season. Christian Grall, the award-winning chef in charge of hospitality at Anfield, says he has the perfect recipe for Christmas pudding, Christmas cake and brandy butter.

Christian, who regularly cooks for football directors, Liverpool FC players and press, says: "When it comes to making your pudding, try and make it two weeks before the big day. Not only does it allow you to tick off the dessert course on your list of things to do, but also, by doing it at this stage, it means the end result is going to taste fantastic."

Serves 4

8oz shredded suet
Half tsp mixed spice
Pinch of cinnamon
2oz self-raising flour
Half lb dark brown sugar
4oz breadcrumbs
10oz currants
4oz raisins
4oz sultanas
1oz chopped nuts (pecans, walnuts or almonds)
1oz mixed peel
Grated rind of orange & 1 lemon
2 eggs, whisked
6oz Guinness
A little brandy

Blend all of the dry ingredients together in a large bowl and then add the sugar, the fruit and all of the liquid ingredients. Try not to over-mix this mixture. Then, put it in a basin and cover it with greaseproof paper and tinfoil (this you can tie around rim.) You then steam this in a double pan for eight hours. After this time, leave it to cool.

Douse it with brandy or sherry (depending on your taste).

Brandy Butter

In a medium-sized bowl, add equal quantities of unsalted butter, icing sugar and cream together until light and fluffy. Add brandy to taste.

Usual amount to serve four people is 3oz of icing sugar with two tablespoons of brandy.

A RIVER REBORN

IT was the river that powered the Industrial Revolution, the heart of the North West's thriving business empire.

But, as industry flourished and the population grew, the rivers of the Mersey Basin suffered. Chronic pollution from industrial discharges and raw sewage brought about a drastic decline in water quality and the life in our rivers.

Dr Keith Hendry of aquatic consultancy firm APEM Ltd, says: "For most of its history, the River Mersey saw mighty annual salmon runs of our own native species, Atlantic Salmon. As late as the 1700s workers on the river complained of having too much fish to eat. That all ended with the terrible poisoning of our environment that accompanied the industrial revolution."

Over the past 25 years, more than £1bn has been invested in cleaning up the Mersey - The Mersey Basin campaign was launched by Michael Heseltine in the wake of the Toxteth riots.

Now, it is considered one of the cleanest in the UK, a situation which is in stark contrast to when it was commonly regarded as the most polluted estuary in Europe. The river's 110 km journey begins at Stockport, where the rivers of the Pennine hills, the Goyt and Tame, come together, and ends at Liverpool Bay where it flows into the Irish Sea.

The Mersey has been reborn and the results are there for all to see - species like salmon and otter have started to return and weirs, installed as part of The Mersey Life Project, have noted trout, chub and eel populations. Regular river workers on the Mersey Ferries even see porpoise and dolphins. There are cod back in the river and, famously, an octopus was recorded at Seacombe.

"Who would have thought back in 1985, at the outset of the Mersey Basin Campaign, that salmon would be breeding in one of the river's headwaters a mere 20 years later?" says Dr Keith Hendry.

"The discovery of young salmon in the River Goyt is a landmark in the restoration of the North West's environment. Perhaps one day we'll see TV pictures of salmon streaming in huge numbers up the River Mersey."

193

Pictures by Colin McPherson

NETTING A FAMILY TRADITION

CHRISTIAN Peet, of Southport Seafoods, has been shrimping since he was five years old.

"The first time I went fishing was with my father who was a part-time shrimper. All the way through my teens I was fishing on my own, I've done it all my life. My brother Kevin and I started the business in 1992 and I've run it on my own for about 15 years.

"I absolutely love it, even though it's not always financially rewarding."

Christian won the 'fish and seafood' category at the Food North West Awards 2009 for his Genuine Southport Potted Shrimps in Butter. The company supplies shrimps, caught off the coast from Crosby to Southport, to several businesses across Merseyside.

Christian's shrimps are all peeled by hand and cooked to his own special recipe, using mace, nutmeg, cayenne pepper and lemon juice before capping them with butter.

"Southport potted shrimps are known all over the country. The recipe dates back to the 1840s. We haven't changed it at all, it's perfect the way it is.

"The best way to eat potted shrimps is to warm them through until the butter melts and serve them with a salad garnish and crusty bread to dip in the butter. It's delicious."

Toast of the town

POTTED SHRIMPS

Lancashire chef and author Tom Bridge has been involved with the history of British cookery for over 30 years, working in television and radio with the BBC. He writes for several local newspapers and enjoys guest appearances in all areas of the catering sector.

Tom says: "Potted shrimps have been popular in the North of England since the 18th century. It was then served as a shrimp tea which consisted of thin slices of white and brown bread, spread with best butter and a bowl of watercress and a pot of strong tea. Today we toast the brown bread and serve the potted shrimps with a wedge of lemon and use it to accompany other fish dishes.

"I make my potted shrimps fresh, and while they are hot, put them onto crisp buttered brown toast, crumpets, cottage loaf or oven-baked, thinly-sliced French stick drizzled with extra virgin olive oil. Another wonderful flavour is sitting thin slices of avocado pear on the base of a hot buttered crumpet, drizzled with lemon or lime juice and topped with warm potted shrimps."

Serves 6
250g butter
450g peeled shrimps
Half tsp powdered mace
Half tsp cayenne pepper
Salt & freshly milled black pepper
Clarified butter

Melt the butter over a moderate heat. Add the shrimps, mace, cayenne and season with salt and freshly milled black pepper. Heat gently but do not boil, stirring them all the time for 5 minutes. Remove from the heat and put them into small cocotte dishes. Seal the tops of the potted shrimps with the clarified butter. Leave the shrimps to chill for at least 2 hours in the fridge. Or serve them warm with Tom's toast suggestions.

To Clarify Butter
Put 225g butter into a saucepan and place it onto a low heat. Skim off the foam as the butter heats. Leave the butter for 10 minutes. Remove the pan from the heat and let it stand for 8 minutes. This ensures that the sediment from the butter stays at the bottom of the saucepan. Carefully pour the butter over the potted shrimps with a large spoon.

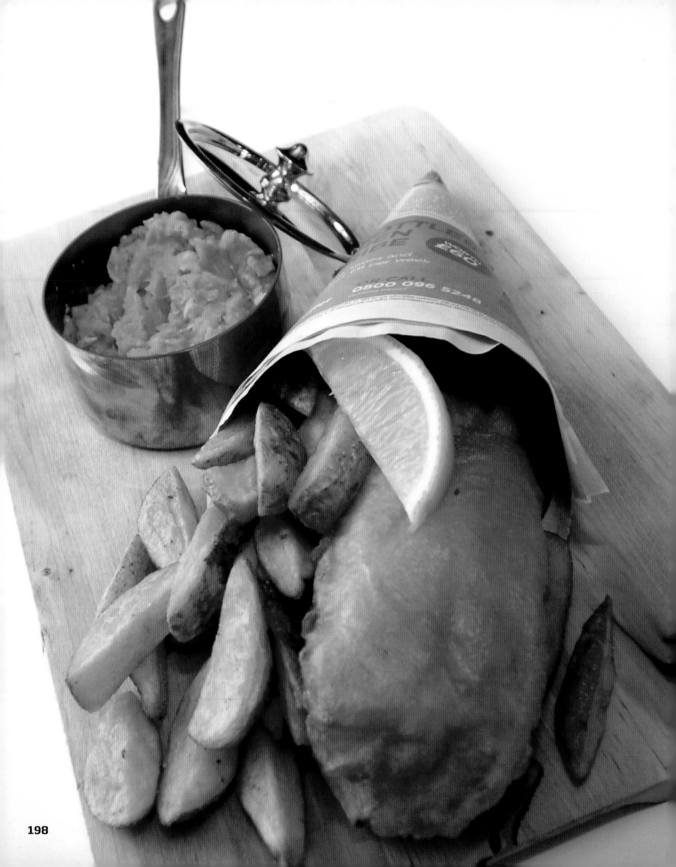

Maritime tradition

FISH AND CHIPS

When it comes to traditional British dishes fish and chips is still a firm favourite. Served in thousands of chip shops across the land since the 19th century, versions can also be found on many a gourmet menu and it is one of many fish-based main courses available at Liverpool's Maritime Dining Rooms.

Here, Nigel Paul Smith, the restaurant's executive chef, offers up his take on the classic. Nigel recommends using coley rather than cod as it's more sustainable, and insists that you make traditional mushy peas to accompany it.

Says Nigel: "Fish and chips has been the backbone of family life in our country since World War II. If you talk to anybody about fish and chips they will immediately draw up from their memory bank the best ever fish and chip shop they have been to.

"This was the inspiration for my dish, to try and recreate those warm comforting feelings. We did this by analysing what was great about fish and chips – the parts of it people loved, crispy chips with a light, tasty, crispy batter and, of course, moreish mushy peas!"

Serves 4
600g coley
2kg chipped potatoes

For the batter
200ml bitter
6g sugar
2 eggs
280g plain flour
20ml iced water

For the mushy peas
120g marrowfat peas
1 litre water

Combine all batter ingredients and whisk to add air.
Trim the fish to make sure you have even portions with no waste; it should be around 150g per portion. Place the fish in seasoned flour, then into the batter gently (not destroying the air you have in the batter), lightly coat the fish and place into a deep-fat fryer at 180°C and cook for 5-6 minutes or until the batter has set.

To make the mushy peas, place the peas and water in a pressure cooker and cook for 25 minutes check at 20 minutes to make sure they are not over cooked. Once cooked, season and serve.

Blanch the chips at 140°C for 7-8 minutes or until soft, leave to cool naturally then finish in the fryer at 200°C until crisp.

Marmite delight

Nigel Paul Smith, executive chef at The Maritime Dining Rooms, says: "This dish is all about getting the best out of a great local ingredient while concentrating on precise cooking, balanced flavours and nice textures, simply pan-fry and finish with five or six drops of lemon juice to bring out the best in the fish."

PAN-FRIED BRILL

Serves 2
2 X 140g brill portion
4 shallots
80g butter
100g soft brown sugar

For the potatoes
250g potatoes
70g butter
150g Marmite

Cook the peeled shallots in an oven at 180°C for 50 minutes with the sugar and butter.

Peel the potatoes and use a small scoop or melon baller to Parisienne them into small balls. Cook for 6-7 minutes in a pan with a little olive oil or until slightly undercooked.

Clean the brill, removing any excess skin or flank flesh. Pan-fry for about 3-4 minutes on the presentation side in butter and oil, and a minute on the other side.

Finish the potatoes in a frying pan with the butter until golden, then add the Marmite and lightly coat and season.

Italian Club style

COZZE ALL MARINARA

Cozze all marinara, or mussels marinara style, is a popular dish across Europe but in Italy the dish is distinguished by the use of tomatoes and chilli in the marinade, rather than cream. "This is a very Italian style of cooking fish," explains Maurizio Pellegrini, head chef at The Italian Club Fish.

"You can eat this as a starter or increase the amount for a main course. We ate it a lot as a family with nice juicy mussels from the Adriatic. I grew up with it as mussels were very cheap and the cherry tomatoes grow in your garden! We'd do a huge pan of it!"

Serves 2-3

500g mussels - washed and scrubbed, discard the open ones
3 cloves of garlic
Extra virgin olive oil
50g chopped parsley
Glass of white wine
100g cherry tomatoes
Half a red chilli
Pinch of salt

Take a deep pan and pour in four tablespoons of olive oil – enough to cover the bottom of the pan. When warmed, add the chopped garlic. When the garlic has browned, add the mussels. After 2 minutes, add the sliced chilli and the cherry tomatoes which have been cut in half. Put the lid on the pan.

After 2-3 minutes the mussels should start to open. Add the wine and cook for a further 5-6 minutes on a medium heat. Season to taste. Serve with a toasted ciabatta rubbed with garlic.

Simon passes the taste test

SALMON BURGERS
FISH PIE

Simon Rimmer made good food the order of the day at Liverpool Women's hospital, after he was approached by staff to help enhance meal times for all its patients. This involved creating a healthy, balanced meal plan involving meat, fish and vegetarian choices.

When it came to selecting fish recipes that would be suitable for the 200 patients, the Something-for-the-Weekend star opted for delicious salmon burgers and tasty fish pie.

Simon says: "We needed recipes that were easy to make in the hospital kitchens so they could be produced en masse for hundreds of patients every day. This means they are also quick and easy for families to make at home. For the fish pie, make sure all the fish and vegetables are kept nice and chunky, don't chop them up too small. There's nothing worse than a fish pie when you can't see where the fish ends and the mash starts.

"This also means the recipe is more nutritious as the ingredients aren't cooked to within an inch of their lives. For the fish cakes, they are about half and half fish and potato which provides a nice texture and a fantastic flavour."

Salmon Burgers

Serves 8
600g skinless salmon cut into chunks, 100g mashed potato, 100g grated raw potato, 1 finely chopped shallot, 1tsp salt, Half tsp black pepper

To serve: 8 focaccia buns, lettuce leaf and sliced tomato, 1 tsp mayonnaise per bun

Place the salmon and shallot in a processor and pulse until combined but not a puree. Tip the salmon into a bowl and mix in the potato. Season with the salt and pepper. Divide the mixture into eight and shape into burgers. Chill for at least 30 minutes.

Grill or oven bake until golden brown and completely cooked through. To serve, place a lettuce leaf and three slices of tomato onto one side of the bun. Place a salmon burger and one teaspoon of mayonnaise on top.

Fish Pie

Serves 5
500g mashed spuds (about 50g butter in the spuds), 750g assorted fish (salmon, pollock, smoked haddock), 1 chopped onion, 1 crushed garlic clove, parsley, 2 chopped leeks, about 350g prepared béchamel sauce, 1 tbsp peas, 1 tbsp capers

Fry the onion and leek with the garlic until soft. Add the fish and sauce, peas, capers and herb. Spoon into individual dishes, spoon on the mash, cook for about 20 minutes at 180°C.

Salmon Burgers

Noble catch of the day

SALMON WITH CHICKPEAS AND SPICED PIQUILLO HARISSA

The Noble House's head chef, Dave Critchley, has three different varieties of freshly caught fish delivered to the restaurant every day.

"As well as the variety of fish dishes available from the a la carte menu, we also offer daily specials. Our fish is carefully selected after consulting my fish supplier for the best quality and value available," says Dave.

"The first dish I have prepared is organic Scottish salmon with crushed, scented chickpeas and spiced piquillo harissa. The chickpea and harissa garnish is a unique Moroccan-inspired flavour."

Serves 4

For the Harissa
Six red chillies, roughly chopped
1tsp roasted cumin seeds
1tsp roasted caraway seeds
1tsp paprika hot smoked
Grated zest of quarter a lemon
1 clove fresh garlic
4 piquillo peppers chopped into bite size pieces
1tsp of rice wine vinegar
Salt and fresh milled black pepper
2 dessertspoons of tomato puree

For the Chickpeas
400g cooked chickpeas, lightly crushed
4 sprigs coriander
2 whole spring onions, sliced into thin strips
Good pinch of chopped flat parsley
1 roasted red pepper, finely chopped
1 clove of fresh garlic, crushed
3 dessertspoon olive oil
Pinch of ground coriander
Salt and freshly milled black pepper
1 tsp rice wine vinegar
Pinch of hot smoked paprika
Pinch of turmeric

For the Salmon
Four organic salmon 6oz portions (skin on bones removed)
100g wild rocket leaves
Maldon sea salt flakes
Fresh milled black pepper

For the Harissa
Place the roasted cumin and caraway seeds into a mortar and pestle and grind to a powder. Place all the ingredients into a food processor and blend to a fine puree. Add a dash of extra virgin olive oil. Place into a suitable container, cover, keep in the fridge until needed.

For the Chickpeas
Lightly crush the chickpeas. Place all the prepared ingredients into a mixing bowl and toss together. Cover and refrigerate.

For the Salmon
Heat a non-stick pan over a medium heat. Lightly oil the salmon with some olive oil and season to your taste. Carefully place the salmon, skin side down, into the hot pan and cook for approx four minutes over a low to medium heat, you will be able to see the fish cooking, so cook till half way up the portion then gently turn over and repeat the process.

Good quality salmon should be cooked slightly pink in the centre. If this is your preference, then a cook time of approximately six to eight minutes will suffice, if you prefer it a little more well done, continue to cook completely through. Once cooked remove from the pan.

Place the crushed chickpeas into a suitable dish and microwave, this will be the easiest way to reheat, check that they are piping hot. Once both hot products are ready, plate, split the chickpeas equally between the four dishes and add rocket leaves.

Sit the hot salmon to one side of the rocket and serve as much harissa as you desire, drizzle some extra virgin olive oil over the rocket leaves and sprinkle a couple of sea salt flakes on top. Garnish with some fresh coriander and serve immediately.

Rings of fire

SOY AND CHILLI MARINATED CALAMARI

The Noble House's head chef Dave Critchley, says: "This dish is representative of some of the small 'taster' dishes we serve."

Serves 2

6 baby squid (frozen), 25ml soy sauce, half a red chilli, one small thumb of fresh ginger, 50ml rice wine vinegar, 4 dessert spoons of extra virgin olive oil, 10g fresh coriander, 1 clove fresh garlic, 1 spring onion, zest and juice of half a lime, 30ml honey, freshly milled pepper

Slit each squid down its body and open out flat, scrape residues, finely score in a crisscross manner on the inside of the body, remove the beak from the head and cut in half.

Slice the red chilli into very thin rings. Peel and grate the ginger and garlic. Slice the spring onion very thinly.

Place all the ingredients except the squid, olive oil and fresh pepper into a mixing bowl and mix together. Heat a ribbed skillet pan over a very high heat until almost at smoking point. Lightly season the squid with the fresh pepper and about 3 tablespoons of olive oil. Place scored side down onto the hot skillet and cook for approximately one minute – no longer otherwise it will become chewy (also cook the squid heads in the same way).

Once cooked and whilst, hot add to the mixing bowl and toss together. This recipe is best placed into a suitable container, put into the fridge and left to marinate for at least 24hrs (no more than 48hrs).

To serve allow the squid to come up to room temperature and garnish with fresh coriander leaves – if using on a later date keep no longer than three days in the fridge.

FAMOUS ICE-CREAM

FLA

* PANAC
* VANIL
* CHOCO
* COFFEE
* MINT
* RUM R
* TUTTI
* HAZELA

NICHOLLs
OF
PARKGATE

Wafer Cones
MediumCone   £1.30
LargeCone   £1.50
Twin Cone   £2.20

Waffle Cones   Plain Chocolate
Scoop Waffle Cone   £1.50 £1.60
Scoop Waffle Cone   £2.50 £2.70
Scoop Waffle Cone   £3.00 £3.30

TUBS
Medium Tub (2 scoops)   £1.60
1/2 Litre Tub   £2.50
1 Litre Tub   £3.70
                              85p
Childs Cone / Tub   £1.50
Gluten Free Cone   £1.50
Sandwich Waffer

ICE-CREAM TEAM HAVE AWARD RIVALS LICKED

IF you visit Parkgate on a summer afternoon, you're bound to see a snake-like queue winding its way out of the shop door at Nicholls of Parkgate.

This award-winning business has been making ice-cream on the premises since 1937 and is a much-loved Wirral institution. For the past 22 years, Nicholls has been owned by Bill Collier, who, using knowledge gained through running a West African Merchants in Liverpool, saw Nicholls as a new venture and a challenge to stretch his already experienced business acumen.

Says Bill: "I immediately saw the potential that Nicholls offered. Although I had no ice-cream making experience, with a short course at Reading University in the Manufacture of Ice-cream, I used my knowledge of running my own business and transferred those skills to the world of ice-cream."

The leap of faith has certainly paid off, with Bill and his team serving tens of thousands of ice-creams a year.

Having updated the equipment with new machines bought from Italy - the home of ice-cream making - Bill has seen the process improve and the quality of his products rise.

Continues Bill: "Nicholls started in 1937 and was owned by a local farmer. He used the milk from his herd of cows to produce the ice-cream.

"We've continued to build on this success by investing in new equipment such as pasteurizers and freezers and sourcing our flavours from the best suppliers in Italy."

Hidden in the back is where the heart of Nicholls beats. This is where the flavours are blended and the ice-cream and sorbets are mixed.

Helen Wilson is the woman behind the ice-cream cones. It is Helen who painstakingly mixes the ice-cream, making hundreds of litres, ready to serve to eager customers.

Helen even gets to experiment with new flavours and has created some unusual blends including apple pie, vanilla with pork scratchings and pinapple and basil sorbet.

Nicholls' reputation is so strong, that local restaurants, such as the Marsh Cat, Mr Chows and the Boat House, have been offering its ice-cream on their dessert menus.

This local gem has even fought off stiff competition to win an array of awards from the Ice-cream Alliance, which holds national competitions annually.

For Bill it's the weather that holds the key. Watching the weather forecast on a daily basis, determines how much ice-cream is made, how many staff are brought in and, of course, how much ice-cream is sold.

Nicholls of Parkgate has been delighting customers for over 70 years, and long may it continue!

Hanover Street, home of chocolate

STRAWBERRY, CHOCOLATE AND CHAMPAGNE SOUP

You'd think someone who runs a chocolatier would have had a life-long obsession with chocolate, but Bala Croman never really used to eat a lot of it. Then, one day, she tried 'real' chocolate at a food festival and became hooked!

Inspired by the film, Chocolat, the former commodities trader opened The Chocolate Cellar on Hanover Street in 2008. Bala has designed this recipe as a refreshing summer dessert. To serve it in winter, swap the white chocolate with dark, and use a couple of shots of Tia Maria instead of Champagne.

The Chocolate Cellar uses Belgian chocolate for its rich, velevety taste, and Venezuelan dark chocolate as it's quite a raw chocolate and really tastes of the cocoa beans. You can buy both Belgian and Venezuelan chocolate bars, which are ideal for cooking, from The Chocolate Cellar.

Serves 4
100ml of single cream
Half a punnet of strawberries (about 200g)
100ml Champagne or sparkling wine
200g white chocolate

Chop up the strawberries and puree them. Bring the cream to the boil, or until it is scalding hot. Mix the strawberry puree and cream together, then sieve it to create a nice smooth puree.

Add 200g of melted white chocolate and the Champagne or sparkling wine. For added flavour, Bala suggests adding either a pinch of black pepper or grated lime zest. Serve in espresso cups.

Back at old school
VICTORIA SPONGE

With afternoon tea and retro-baking now officially back in vogue, executive chef at the Maritime Dining Rooms, Nigel Paul Smith, has made a conscious effort to incorporate some old-school cake recipes into his cooking. This recipe for a traditional Victoria sandwich cake is a proper teatime treat.

To whisk the eggs and sugar like a pro, Nigel advises: "The key to whisking is a consistent technique, not going at it hell for leather, and you need to achieve a figure of eight action."

Makes a 10-inch cake
5 eggs
60g melted butter
150g caster sugar
150g plain flour
6-7 tbsps strawberry jam,
284ml double cream
Icing sugar for dusting

Pre-heat the oven to 190°C. Put a pan of water on to simmer and gently warm the eggs and caster sugar in a large bowl that fits comfortably over the pan. Whisk the eggs and sugar until the sugar begins to dissolve. Take off the heat and whisk until cool – the mixture will double and, if you whisk really well, it will treble.

Gently fold in the flour over five stages, being careful not to knock out the air you've just whisked in. Next, add the molten butter and fold in gradually. Line a 10-inch baking tin with greaseproof paper. Place greaseproof paper around the inside edge of the tin too, using a little oil on the tin to help it stick. Slowly and gently add the cake mix to the tin. Bake for 15-20 mins. Once the sponge is cooked, allow to cool then slice in half through the middle.

Spread strawberry jam liberally on one half of the cake. Whisk the double cream until thick, then spread on the other half of the cake. Join the two halves together, press gently until the filling oozes to the edge. Dust with icing sugar.

Prayers answered for Lunya

Owner and executive chef of Lunya, Peter Kinsella, says: "I can't take the credit for this recipe. At a charity auction a few years ago, I won the prize of having the then Bishop of Birkenhead cook dinner in my house, and this is what he served for dessert. In the restaurant we serve this with chilli-infused raspberries, but it is just as good with the fruit compote in this recipe."

WHITE CHOCOLATE CHEESECAKE

Serves 8-12

250g of plain digestive biscuits
100g of unsalted butter, melted
250g of mascarpone cheese
300g of soft white cheese
300g of double cream
400g of the best white chocolate you can afford to buy (Green and Black's is recommended)

Crush the digestive biscuits finely, bind with the melted butter and press into the bottom of a 20cm spring form cake tin, place in the fridge for at least half an hour to cool.

Mix the mascarpone, soft cheese and cream together, do not whisk, use a fork and gently mix until they are smooth.

Melt the white chocolate and add it to the cream and cheese mixture, folding gently until it is well mixed.

Add the white chocolate and cream mixture to the cake tin and smooth over the top.

Place in the fridge for four hours, or, even better, overnight to allow the flavours to intensify.

Serve either plain, or with a fresh fruit compote. Try gently braising strawberries in Champagne, remove the strawberries, add a tiny amount of arrowroot to the liquid and boil the mixture to the required thickness, put the strawberries back in and pour this over each slice of cheesecake.

Rustic pud
a winner

MINT CREME
BRULEE

Serves 6

375ml double or whipping cream
200ml milk (semi or whole)
20g picked mint leaves (small handful)
8 medium egg yolks
75g caster sugar and a little extra to
sprinkle on top

Paul Fuller, head chef at The James Monro in Liverpool, tells us: "This is our signature rustic dessert which is one of my own favourites.

"To make the dessert a bit different, I experiment with an array of ever changing flavours so customers can experience a new taste sensation whenever they visit. The Mint Crème Brulee offers a treat at the end of any meal, with a delicate hint of mint which offers a divine and refreshing treat on the palette."

Bring milk, cream and mint leaves to boil in a pan and remove from heat. Whisk sugar and eggs together and add a little of the milk and the cream to the mixture and mix well and pour back into the pan with the rest of the milk and cream and stir well. Leave to infuse for 30 mins. Strain mixture into jug.

Heat oven to 150°C (130°C if fan assisted). Place 6-8 125ml ramekins into a roasting dish and fill half of the way up with the brulee mix. Fill the roasting dish with boiling water about half way up the ramekins.

Cover with foil and place into oven and cook for about 40-45 minutes. (The brulees will be done if, when you tap them they still wobble in the middle. If not leave them in for another 5-10 minutes and check again. Take out of tray and leave to cool for one hour. Refrigerate for 2-3 hours.

To serve, place a little bit of caster sugar on top and gently blow torch until the sugar has dissolved. If you don't have a blow torch place under a hot grill, but make sure you keep an eye on it as it can caramelise quite quickly.

Room for a treat

There's nothing easier than a lemon posset recipe for a quick, and deliciously tangy pudding.

John O'Brien, head chef at The Living Room, serves this summery pud in 220ml glass dessert dishes, but you can easily substitute for ramekins, small glasses or espresso cups.

LEMON AND BLACKBERRY POSSET

Serves 6
150g blackberries
600ml double cream
2 lemons
150g caster sugar

Pour the cream and caster sugar into a saucepan. Zest and juice the lemons. Add the lemon zest and juice to the cream and sugar. Over a moderate heat bring the cream to the boil. Reduce the heat and simmer for 5 minutes, stirring occasionally to avoid the cream catching on the bottom of the pan.

Remove the pan from the heat and allow to cool slightly. Divide the blackberries between the 6 X 220ml glass dessert dishes. Ensure that the blackberries remain at the edge of the pot so they can be seen.

Divide the cream mix equally between the six dishes, pouring over the blackberries gently so not to move them. Place in the fridge for 1 to 2 hrs to set. Serve with lavender shortbread.

THE LIVERPOOL COOKBOOK
Recipe Directory

THE LIVERPOOL COOKBOOK
Restaurant Directory

60 Hope Street
Hope Street, Liverpool
0151 707 6060

The Academy
Tradewind Square, Liverpool
0151 252 4512

Alma De Cuba
Seel Street, Liverpool
0151 702 7394

Barburrito
Liverpool ONE, Liverpool
0151 708 5085

Blackburne House Café Bar
Blackburne Place, Liverpool
0151 708 3929

Blakes
North John Street, Liverpool
0151 243 2121

Bistro Franc
Hanover Street, Liverpool
0151 708 9993

The Buffet Club
Prescot Street, Liverpool
0151 260 6660

Chaophraya
Kenyon Steps, Liverpool
0151 707 6323

The Chocolate Cellar
Hanover Street, Liverpool
0151 709 5197

Christakis
York Street, Liverpool
0151 708 7377

Delifonseca
Stanley Street, Liverpool
0151 255 0808

Etsu
The Strand, Liverpool
0151 236 7530

Everyman Bistro
Hope Street, Liverpool
0151 708 9545

Fraiche
Rose Mount, Prenton
0151 652 2914

The Gulshan
Aigburth Road, Liverpool
0151 427 2273

Gusto
Albert Dock, Liverpool
0151 708 6969

Heathcotes
Beetham Plaza, Liverpool
0151 236 3536

HOST
Hope Street, Liverpool
0151 708 5831

Il Forno
Duke Street, Liverpool
0151 709 4002

The Italian Club
Bold Street, Liverpool
0151 708 5508

Italian Club Fish
Bold Street, Liverpool
0151 707 2110

The James Monro
Tithebarn Street, Liverpool
0151 236 9700

Julian's Restaurant
Birkenhead Road, Hoylake
0151 632 6241

Las Iguanas
Liverpool ONE, Liverpool
0151 709 4030

La Vina
North John Street, Liverpool
0151 255 1401

Lenny's Bar & Grill
Sir Thomas Street, Liverpool
0151 227 1079

Little Green Café
Aigburth Road, Liverpool
0151 727 6515

The Living Room
Victoria Street, Liverpool
0151 236 1999

The London Carriage Works
Hope Street, Liverpool
0151 705 2222

Lunya
College Lane, Liverpool
0151 706 9770

Maggie May's
Bold Street, Liverpool
0151 709 7600

Malmaison
Princes Dock, Liverpool
0151 229 5000

Marco Pierre White's The Swan
Aughton, Ormskirk
01695 421 450

Maritime Dining Rooms
Albert Dock, Liverpool
0151 478 4056

Matou
Pier Head, Liverpool
0151 236 2928

Meet Argentinian
Brunswick Street, Liverpool
0151 258 1816

The Noble House
Brunswick Street, Liverpool
0151 236 5346

O'Neill's
Hanover Street, Liverpool
0151 709 7360

Panoramic
Beetham West Tower, Liverpool
0151 236 5534

Peninsula Dining Room
Grosvenor Road, New Brighton
0151 639 8338

The Quarter
Falkner Street, Liverpool
0151 707 1965